AngularJS Test-driven Development

Implement the best practices to improve your AngularJS applications using test-driven development

Tim Chaplin

[PACKT] open source *
PUBLISHING
community experience distilled

BIRMINGHAM - MUMBAI

AngularJS Test-driven Development

First published: January 2015

Production reference: 1230115

Published by Packt Publishing Ltd.
Livery Place
35 Livery Street
Birmingham B3 2PB, UK.

ISBN 978-1-78439-883-5

www.packtpub.com

Credits

Author
Tim Chaplin

Reviewers
Md. Ziaul Haq
Nive Jayasekar
Tim Pei
Andi Smith

Commissioning Editor
Pramila Balan

Acquisition Editor
Reshma Raman

Content Development Editor
Manasi Pandire

Technical Editor
Madhunikita Sunil Chindarkar

Copy Editors
Gladson Monteiro
Adithi Shetty
Stuti Srivastava

Project Coordinator
Leena Purkait

Proofreaders
Simran Bhogal
Maria Gould
Ameesha Green
Paul Hindle

Indexer
Hemangini Bari

Production Coordinator
Aparna Bhagat

Cover Work
Aparna Bhagat

About the Author

Tim Chaplin lives and breathes software solutions and innovations. During the day, he works with Fortune 100 enterprise applications, and in the evening, he perfects his craft by contributing to and distributing open source software, writing, and constantly looking for ways to increase his knowledge of technology and the world. At an early age, Tim began developing software and has been hooked on it since. Tim is an established conference speaker who has extensive experience in developing and leading AngularJS projects. He has a wide background of JavaScript, C#, Java, and C++ languages. Tim specializes in leading code quality and testing throughout all his applications. After attending California State University, Chico, he has gone on to work in Shanghai, Los Angeles, and London.

> I would like to thank my wife, Pierra, for always making me think and dream bigger. I would also like to thank my family for their constant love and support. Pops, this one's for you babe.

About the Reviewers

Md. Ziaul Haq is a senior software engineer from Dhaka, Bangladesh, who has been working with the oDesk core platform development team as a senior JavaScript developer since 2011. He likes to work mostly on the frontend, though he is a full-stack developer. JavaScript is his passion and he likes to code in it all day long. He is well known as *jquerygeek* in the web community.

Md. Ziaul started his career in 2005 as a software developer. He has work experience with UNICEF locally and internationally, where he worked with UNICEF's web CMS. He is currently pursuing a master's degree in computer science from United International University, Dhaka, Bangladesh.

I would like to thank my wife, Richi, and my newborn son, Arabi, who is my inspiration.

Nive Jayasekar started programming in high school. In her last year of high school, she won $10,500 at a Hackathon for building a mobile artificial-intelligence app. She has interned at Facebook and LinkedIn, and will soon graduate from Carnegie Mellon University with a degree in computer science and a minor in machine learning. She is always interested in building game-changing products. She has 5 years of experience building web and mobile applications using Python, AngularJS, Java, and Objective C.

I'd like to thank the people at Packt Publishing, Leena Purkait and Kirti Patil, for their help in producing this book.

Tim Pie is a computer science and business administration double degree student at the University of Waterloo, Ontario. He has gained a wide range of technical skills through past projects and internships, including cloud computing, data mining, and full stack web development. Tim's current technical interest is focusing on building web applications using modern web technologies, specifically HTML5 and web components.

I'd like to thank my parents for their constant support of my pursuits, while providing me great advice along the way.

Andi Smith (@andismith) is a senior architect who specializes in frontend solutions at ideas and innovation agency, AKQA.

Andi has over 15 years of experience building for the Web and has worked with clients such as Nike, Ubisoft, Sainsburys, Barclays, Heineken, and MINI. He has also created a number of open source plugins and sites such as Grunt Responsive Images (http://www.andismith.com/grunt-responsive-images/) and Secrets of the Browser Developer Tools (http://devtoolsecrets.com/).

Andi maintains a blog focused on frontend development at http://www.andismith.com/.

I would like to thank my wife, Amy, for all her love and support.

www.PacktPub.com

Support files, eBooks, discount offers, and more

For support files and downloads related to your book, please visit www.PacktPub.com.

Did you know that Packt offers eBook versions of every book published, with PDF and ePub files available? You can upgrade to the eBook version at www.PacktPub.com and as a print book customer, you are entitled to a discount on the eBook copy. Get in touch with us at service@packtpub.com for more details.

At www.PacktPub.com, you can also read a collection of free technical articles, sign up for a range of free newsletters and receive exclusive discounts and offers on Packt books and eBooks.

https://www2.packtpub.com/books/subscription/packtlib

Do you need instant solutions to your IT questions? PacktLib is Packt's online digital book library. Here, you can search, access, and read Packt's entire library of books.

Why subscribe?

- Fully searchable across every book published by Packt
- Copy and paste, print, and bookmark content
- On demand and accessible via a web browser

Free access for Packt account holders

If you have an account with Packt at www.PacktPub.com, you can use this to access PacktLib today and view 9 entirely free books. Simply use your login credentials for immediate access.

Table of Contents

Preface

The book will provide the reader with a complete guide to the test-driven development (TDD) approach for AngularJS. It will provide step-by-step, clear examples to continually reinforce TDD best practices. The book will look at both unit testing with Karma and end-to-end testing with Protractor. It will not only focus on how to use the tools, but also on understanding the reason they were built, and why they should be used. Throughout, there will be focus on when, where, and how to use these tools, constantly reinforcing the principles of the TDD life cycle (test, execute, refactor).

What this book covers

This book is basically split into two parts. The initial chapters focus on the TDD life cycle, and how Karma and Protractor fit into the life cycle and development of an AngularJS application. As we proceed, you'll get a step-by-step approach to AngularJS TDD using Karma and Protractor. Each of the chapters builds up on the previous one and introduces how to test several different AngularJS components.

Chapter 1, Introduction to Test-driven Development, is an introduction to the concepts of TDD and testing techniques.

Chapter 2, The Karma Way, explores the origins of Karma and why it is an essential tool for any AngularJS project.

Chapter 3, End-to-end Testing with Protractor, introduces the simplicity of Protractor, an end-to-end testing tool built specifically for AngularJS.

Chapter 4, The First Steps, covers the TDD journey and shows the fundamentals and tools in action.

Chapter 5, Flip Flop, expands to include testing for multiple controllers, partial views, location references, CSS, and HTML element building on the initial foundational aspects learned in the previous chapter.

Chapter 6, Telling the World, dives into communicating across controllers, and testing services and broadcasting.

Chapter 7, Give Me Some Data, dives into how to apply several of the concepts shown previously, and extend them to pull data using an external API.

Appendix A, Integrating Selenium Server with Protractor, walks through setting up and configuring Protractor to use a standalone Selenium server.

Appendix B, Automating Karma Unit Testing on Commit, covers how to set up Travis CI, a platform for continuous integration, and setting up Karma to test your application.

Who this book is for

This book is for the developer who wants to go beyond the basic tutorials, and wants to take the plunge into AngularJS development. This book is for the developer who has experience with AngularJS and has walked through the basic tutorials but wants to understand the wider context of when, why, and how to apply testing techniques and best practices to create quality-clean code. To get the most out of this book, it is preferred that the reader has basic understanding of HTML, JavaScript, and AngularJS.

Conventions

In this book, you will find a number of styles of text that distinguish between different kinds of information. Here are some examples of these styles and an explanation of their meaning.

Code words in text, database table names, folder names, filenames, file extensions, pathnames, dummy URLs, user input, and Twitter handles are shown as follows: "Create a web page and import `calculator.js` for testing."

A block of code is set as follows:

```
<!DOCTYPE html>
<html>
<head>
  <title></title>
</head>
<body>
```

```
<script src="calculator.js"></script>
</body>
</html>
```

Any command-line input or output is written as follows:

```
$ node calculator.js
```

New terms and **important words** are shown in bold. Words that you see on the screen, in menus or dialog boxes for example, appear in the text like this: "Traditionally, tests were run by having to manually launch a browser and check for results by continually hitting the **Refresh** button."

> Warnings or important notes appear in a box like this.

> Tips and tricks appear like this.

Reader feedback

Feedback from our readers is always welcome. Let us know what you think about this book—what you liked or disliked. Reader feedback is important for us as it helps us develop titles that you will really get the most out of.

To send us general feedback, simply e-mail feedback@packtpub.com, and mention the book's title in the subject of your message.

If there is a topic that you have expertise in and you are interested in either writing or contributing to a book, see our author guide at www.packtpub.com/authors.

Customer support

Now that you are the proud owner of a Packt book, we have a number of things to help you to get the most from your purchase.

Downloading the example code

You can download the example code files from your account at `http://www.packtpub.com` for all the Packt Publishing books you have purchased. If you purchased this book elsewhere, you can visit `http://www.packtpub.com/support` and register to have the files e-mailed directly to you.

Errata

Although we have taken every care to ensure the accuracy of our content, mistakes do happen. If you find a mistake in one of our books—maybe a mistake in the text or the code—we would be grateful if you could report this to us. By doing so, you can save other readers from frustration and help us improve subsequent versions of this book. If you find any errata, please report them by visiting `http://www.packtpub.com/submit-errata`, selecting your book, clicking on the **Errata Submission Form** link, and entering the details of your errata. Once your errata are verified, your submission will be accepted and the errata will be uploaded to our website or added to any list of existing errata under the Errata section of that title.

To view the previously submitted errata, go to `https://www.packtpub.com/books/content/support` and enter the name of the book in the search field. The required information will appear under the **Errata** section.

Piracy

Piracy of copyright material on the Internet is an ongoing problem across all media. At Packt, we take the protection of our copyright and licenses very seriously. If you come across any illegal copies of our works, in any form, on the Internet, please provide us with the location address or website name immediately so that we can pursue a remedy.

Please contact us at `copyright@packtpub.com` with a link to the suspected pirated material.

We appreciate your help in protecting our authors, and our ability to bring you valuable content.

Questions

You can contact us at `questions@packtpub.com` if you are having a problem with any aspect of the book, and we will do our best to address it.

1
Introduction to Test-driven Development

AngularJS is at the forefront of client-side JavaScript testing. Every AngularJS tutorial includes an accompanying test, and event test modules are part of the core AngularJS package. The Angular team is focused on making testing fundamental to web development.

This chapter introduces you to the fundamentals of test-driven development with AngularJS including:

- An overview of **test-driven development** (TDD)
- The TDD life cycle: test first, make it run, make it better
- Common testing techniques

An overview of TDD

TDD is not used only to develop software. The fundamental principles can be seen in many industries. This section will explore the fundamentals of TDD and how they are applied by a tailor.

Fundamentals of TDD

Know what to code before you code. This may sound cliché, but this is essentially what TDD gives you. TDD begins by defining expectations, then makes you meet the expectations, and finally forces you to refine the changes after the expectations have been met.

Here are a couple of clear benefits of using TDD:

- **Knowing before you code**: A test provides a clear vision of what code needs to do in order to be successful. Setting up tests first allows focus on only components that have been defined in tests.

- **Confidence in refactoring**: Refactoring involves moving, fixing, and changing a project. Tests protect the core logic from refactoring by ensuring that the logic behaves independently of the code structure.

- **Documentation**: Tests define expectations that a particular object or function must meet. The expectation acts as a contract, and can be used to see how a method should or can be used. This makes the code readable and easier to understand.

Measuring success

TDD is not just a software development practice. The fundamental principles are shared by other craftsmen as well. One of these craftsmen is a tailor, whose success depends on precise measurements and careful planning.

Breaking down the steps

Here are the high-level steps a tailor takes to make a suit:

1. **Test first**:
    - Determining the measurements for the suit
    - Having the customer determine the style and material they want for their suit
    - Measuring the customer's arms, shoulders, torso, waist, and legs

2. **Making the cuts**:
    - Measuring the fabric and cut
    - Selecting the fabric based on the desired style
    - Measuring the fabric based on the customer's waist and legs
    - Cutting the fabric based on the measurements

3. **Refactoring**:
   - ° Comparing the resulting product to the expected style, reviewing, and making changes
   - ° Comparing the cut and look to the customer's desired style
   - ° Making adjustments to meet the desired style

4. **Repeating**:
   - ° **Test first**: Determining the measurements for the pants
   - ° **Making the cuts:** Measuring the fabric and making the cuts
   - ° **Refactor:** Making changes based on the reviews

The preceding steps are an example of a TDD approach. The measurements must be taken before the tailor can start cutting up the raw material. Imagine for a moment if the tailor didn't use a test-driven approach and didn't use a measuring tape (testing tool). It would be ridiculous if the tailor started cutting before measuring.

As a developer, do you "cut before measuring"? Would you trust a tailor without a measuring tape? How would you feel about a developer who doesn't test?

Measure twice cut once

The tailor always starts with measurements. What would happen if the tailor made cuts before measuring? What would happen if the fabric was cut too short? How much extra time would go into the tailoring? Measure twice, cut once.

Software developers can choose from an endless amount of approaches to use before starting developing. One common approach is to work off a specification. A documented approach may help in defining what needs to be built; however, without tangible criteria for how to meet a specification, the actual application that gets developed maybe completely different than the specification. With a TDD approach (test first, make it run, and make it better), every stage of the process verifies that the result meets the specification. Think about how a tailor continues to use a measuring tape to verify the suit throughout the process.

TDD embodies a test-first methodology. TDD gives developers the ability to start with a clear goal and write code that will directly meet a specification. Develop like a professional and follow the practices that will help you write quality software.

Diving in

It is time to dive into some actual code. This walk-through will take you through adding the multiplication functionality to a calculator. Remember the TDD life cycle: test first, make it run, and make it better.

Setting up the test

The initial calculator is in a file called `calculator.js` and is initialized as an object as follows:

```
var calculator = {};
```

The test will be run through a web browser using a basic HTML page. Create a web page and import `calculator.js` to test it. Save the web page as `testRunner.html`. To run the test, open a browser and run `testRunner.html`. Here is the code for `testRunner.html`:

```
<!DOCTYPE html>
<html>
<head>
  <title></title>
</head>
<body>

<script src="calculator.js"></script>
</body>
</html>
```

Now that the project is set up, the next step is to create the development to-do list.

Creating a development to-do list

A development to-do list helps organize and focus your tasks. It also provides a place to write down ideas during the development process.

Here is the initial step for creating a development to-do list:

*   Add multiplication functionality: *3 * 3 = 9*

The preceding list describes what needs to be done. It also provides a clear example of how to verify multiplication: *3 * 3 = 9*.

Test first

Although you can write the multiplication function quickly, remember that once the habit of TDD is set in place, it will be just as quick to write the test and code. Here are the steps for the first test:

1. Open `calculator.js`.

2. Create a new function to test multiplying *3 * 3*:

```
function multipleTest1(){
  //Test
  var result = calculator.multiply(3,3);

  //Assert Result is expected
  if (result === 9) {
    console.log('Test Passed');
  }
  else{
    console.log('Test Failed');
  }
};
```

The test calls a `multiply` function, which still needs to be defined. It then asserts that the results are as expected by displaying a pass or fail message. Remember, in TDD, you are looking at the use of the method and explicitly writing how it should be used. This allows you to define the interface through a use case, as opposed to only looking at the limited scope of the function being developed.

The next step in the TDD life cycle will be focused on making the test run.

Making it run

This step is about making the test run, just as the tailor did with the suit. The measurements were taken during the test step, and now the application can be molded to fit the measurements. Here are the steps to run the test:

1. Open the browser with `testRunner.html`.

2. Open the JavaScript developer **Console** window.

The test throws an error, as shown in the following screenshot:

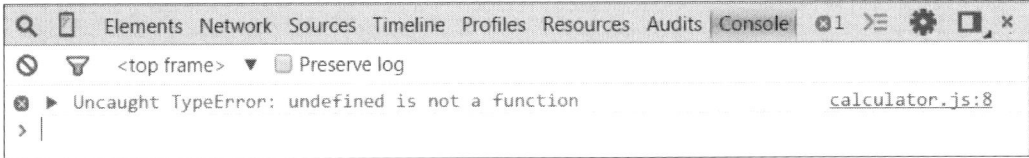

The error thrown is expected as the calculator application calls a function that hasn't been created yet: `calculator.multiply`.

In TDD, the focus is on adding the smallest change to get a test to pass. There is no need to actually implement the multiplication logic. This may seem unintuitive. The point is once a passing test exists, it should always pass. When a method contains fairly complex logic, it is easier to run a passing test against it to ensure it meets the expectations.

What is the smallest change that can be made to make the test pass? By returning the expected value of 9, the test should pass. Although this won't add the `multiply` function, it will confirm the application wiring. In addition, after you have passed the test, making future changes will be easy as you have to simply keep the test passing!

Now, add the `multiply` function and have it return the required value 9:

```
var calculator = {
  multiply : function(){
    return 9;
  }
};
```

In the browser, the JavaScript console reruns the test. The result should be as follows:

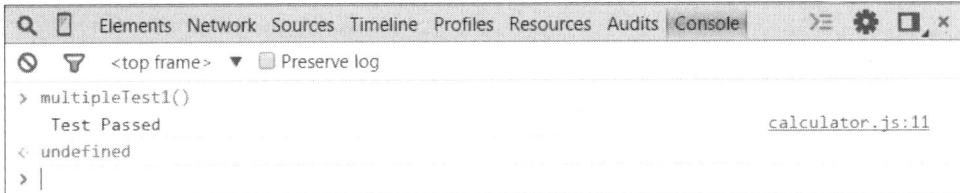

Yes! The test passed. Time to cross out the first item from the to-do list:

- Add multiplication functionality: *3 * 3 = 9*

Now that there is a passing test, the next step will be to remove the hardcoded value in the `multiply` function.

Making it better

The refactoring step needs to remove the hardcoded `return` value of the `multiply` function. The required logic is as follows:

```
var calculator = {
multiply : function(amount1,amount2){
   return amount1 * amount2;
  }
};
```

Rerun the tests and confirm the test passes. Excellent! Now the `multiply` function is complete. Here is the full code for the calculator and test:

```
var calculator = {
  multiply : function(amount1,amount2){
    return amount1* amount2;
  }
};

var multipleTest1 = function (){
  var result = calculator.multiply(3,3);

  if (result === 9) {
    console.log('Test Passed');
  }
  else{
    console.log('Test Failed');
  }

};

multipleTest1();
```

Testing techniques

It is important to understand some fundamental techniques and approaches to testing. This section will walk you through a couple of examples of techniques that will be leveraged in this book. This includes:

- Testing doubles with Jasmine spies
- Refactoring
- Building patterns

In addition, here are additional terms that will be used:

- **Function under test**: This is the function being tested. It is also referred to as system under test, object under test, and so on.

- **The 3 A's (Arrange, Act, and Assert)**: This is a technique used to set up tests, first described by Bill Wake (`http://xp123.com/articles/3a-arrange-act-assert/`). The 3 A's will be discussed further in *Chapter 2, The Karma Way*.

Testing with a framework

Although a simple web page can be used to perform tests, as seen earlier in this chapter, it is much easier to use a testing framework. A testing framework provides methods and structures to test. This includes a standard structure to create and run tests, the ability to create assertions/expectations, the ability to use test doubles, and more. This book uses Jasmine as the test framework. Jasmine is a behavior-driven testing framework. It is highly compatible with testing AngularJS applications. In *Chapter 2, The Karma Way*, we will take a more in-depth look at Jasmine.

Testing doubles with Jasmine spies

A test double is an object that acts and is used in place of another object. Take a look at the following object that needs to be tested:

```
var objectUnderTest = {
  someFunction : function(){}
};
```

Using a test double, you can determine the number of times `someFunction` gets called. Here is an example:

```
var objectUnderTest = {
  someFunction : function(){}
};

jasmine.spyOn(objectUnderTest,'someFunction');

objectUnderTest.someFunction ();
objectUnderTest.someFunction();

console.log(objectUnderTest.someFunction.count);
```

The preceding code creates a test double using a Jasmine spy (`jasmine.spyOn`). The test double is then used to determine the number of times `someFunction` gets called. A Jasmine test double offers the following features and more:

- The count of calls on a function
- The ability to specify a return value (stub a return value)
- The ability to pass a call to the underlying function (pass through)

Throughout this book, you will gain further experience in the use of test doubles.

Stubbing a return value

The great thing about using a test double is that the underlying code of a method does not have to be called. With a test double, you can specify exactly what a method should return for a given test. Here is an example function:

```
var objectUnderTest = {
  someFunction : function(){ return 'stub me!'; }
};
```

The preceding object (`objectUnderTest`) has a function (`someFunction`) that needs to be stubbed. Here is how you can stub the return value using Jasmine:

```
jasmine.spyOn(objectUnderTest,'someFunction')
.and
.returnValue('stubbed value');
```

Now, when `objectUnderTest.someFunction` is called, `stubbed value` will be returned. Here is how the preceding stubbed value can be confirmed using `console.log`:

```
var objectUnderTest = {
  someFunction : function(){ return 'stub me!'; }
};

//before the return value is stubbed
Console.log(objectUnderTest.someFunction());
//displays 'stub me'

jasmine.spyOn(objectUnderTest,'someFunction')
.and
.returnValue('stubbed value');

//After the return value is stubbed
Console.log(objectUnderTest.someFunction());
//displays 'stubbed value'
```

Testing arguments

A test double provides insights into how a method is used in an application. As an example, a test might want to assert what arguments a method was called with or the number of times a method was called. Here is an example function:

```
var objectUnderTest = {
  someFunction : function(arg1,arg2){}
};
```

Here are the steps to test the arguments the preceding function is called with:

1. Create a spy so that the arguments called can be captured:

   ```
   jasmine.spyOn(objectUnderTest,'someFunction');
   ```

2. Then to access the arguments, do the following:

   ```
   //Get the arguments for the first call of the function
   var callArgs = objectUnderTest.someFunction.call.argsFor(0);

   console.log(callArgs);
   //displays ['param1','param2']
   ```

3. Here is how the arguments can be displayed using `console.log`:

   ```
   var objectUnderTest = {
     someFunction : function(arg1,arg2){}
   };

   //create the spy
   jasmine.spyOn(objectUnderTest,'someFunction');

   //Call the method with specific arguments
   objectUnderTest.someFunction('param1','param2');

   //Get the arguments for the first call of the function
   var callArgs = objectUnderTest.someFunction.call.argsFor(0);

   console.log(callArgs);
   //displays ['param1','param2']
   ```

Refactoring

Refactoring is the act of restructuring, rewriting, renaming, and removing code in order to improve the design, readability, maintainability, and overall aesthetic of a piece of code. The TDD life cycle step of "making it better" is primarily concerned with refactoring. This section will walk you through a refactoring example. Here is an example of a function that needs to be refactored:

```
var abc = function(z){
  var x = false;
  if(z > 10)
    return true;


  return x;
}
```

This function works fine and does not contain any syntactical or logical issues. The problem is that the function is difficult to read and understand. Refactoring this function will improve the naming, structure, and definition. The exercise will remove the masquerading complexity and reveal the function's true meaning and intention. Here are the steps:

1. Rename the function and variable names to be more meaningful, that is, rename x and z so that they make sense:

```
var isTenOrGreater = function(value){
  var falseValue = false;
  if(value > 10)
    return true;


  return falseValue;
}
```

2. Now, the function can easily be read and the naming makes sense.

3. Remove unnecessary complexity. In this case, the if conditional statement can be removed completely:

```
var isTenOrGreater = function(value){
  return value > 10;
};
```

4. Reflect on the result.

   At this point, the refactor is complete, and the function's purpose should jump out at you. The remaining question that should be asked is "why does this method exist in the first place?".

This example only provided a brief walk-through of the steps that can be taken to identify issues in code and how to improve them. Other examples will be used throughout this book.

Building with a builder

The builder pattern uses a `builder` object to create another object. Imagine an object with ten properties. How will test data be created for every property? Will the object have to be recreated in every test?

A `builder` object defines an object to be reused across multiple tests. The following code snippet provides an example of the use of this pattern. This example will use `builder` object in the `validate` method:

```
var book = {
   id : null,
   author : null,
   dateTime : null
};
```

The `book` object has three properties: `id`, `author`, and `dateTime`. From a testing perspective, you would want the ability to create a valid object, that is, one that has all the fields defined. You may also want to create an invalid object with missing properties, or you may want to set certain values in the object to test the validation logic, that is, `dateTime` is an actual date.

Here are the steps to create a builder for the `dateTime` object:

1. Create a builder function:

   ```
   var bookBuilder = function();
   ```

2. Create a valid object within the builder:

   ```
   var bookBuilder = function(){
     var _resultBook = {
       id: 1,
       author: 'Any Author',
       dateTime: new DateTime()
     };

   }
   ```

3. Create a function to return the built object:

```
var bookBuilder = function(){
  var _resultBook = {
    id: 1,
    author: "Any Author",
    dateTime: new DateTime()
  };
  this.build = function(){
    return _resultBook;
  }
}
```

4. Create another function to set the `_resultBook` author field:

```
var bookBuilder = function(){
var _resultBook = {
    id: 1,
    author: 'Any Author',
    dateTime: new DateTime()
  };
  this.build = function(){
    return _resultBook;
  };
  this.setAuthor = function(author){
    _resultBook.author = author;
  };
};
```

5. Make the function fluent so that calls can be chained:

```
this.setAuthor = function(author){
  _resultBook.author = author;
  return this;
};
```

6. A setter function will also be created for `dateTime`:

```
this.setDateTime = function(dateTime){
  _resultBook.dateTime = dateTime;
  return this;
};
```

Now, `bookBuilder` can be used to create a new book as follows:

```
var builtBook = bookBuilder.setAuthor('Tim Chaplin')
.setDateTime(new Date())
.build();
```

The preceding builder can now be used throughout your tests to create a single consistent object. Here is the complete builder for your reference:

```
var bookBuilder = function(){
  var _resultBook = {
    id: 1,
    author: 'Any Author',
    dateTime: new DateTime()
  };

  this.build = function(){
    return _resultBook;
  };

  this.setAuthor = function(author){
    _resultBook.author = author;
    return this;
  };

  this.setDateTime = function(dateTime){
    _resultBook.dateTime = dateTime;
    return this;
  };
};
```

Self-test questions

Q1. A test double is another name for a duplicate test.

1. True
2. False

Q2. TDD stands for test-driven development.

1. True
2. False

Q3. The purpose of refactoring is to improve code quality.

1. True
2. False

Q4. A test object builder consolidates the creation of objects for testing.

1. True
2. False

Q5. The 3 A's are a sports team.

1. True
2. False

Summary

This chapter provided an introduction to TDD. It discussed the TDD life cycle (test first, make it run, make it better) and showed how the same steps are used by a tailor. Finally, it looked over some of the testing techniques that will be discussed throughout this book including:

- Test doubles
- Refactoring
- Building patterns

Although TDD is a huge topic, this book is solely focused on the TDD principles and practices to be used with AngularJS. In the next chapter, you will start the journey and see how to set up the Karma test runner.

2
The Karma Way

JavaScript testing has hit the mainstream, thanks to Karma. Karma makes it seamless to test JavaScript. AngularJS was created around testing. This chapter explores the origins of Karma and why it has to be used in any AngularJS project. By the end of this chapter, you will not only understand the problem that Karma solves, but also walk through a complete example using it.

JavaScript testing tools

Knowing what the different testing tools are is half the battle. In this section, you will learn about the two primary tools that will be discussed and used throughout the book. They are:

- **Karma**: This is a test runner
- **Protractor**: This is an end-to-end testing framework

Karma

Before discussing what Karma is, it is best to discuss what it isn't. It isn't a framework to write tests. It is a test runner. What this means is that Karma gives you the ability to run tests in several different browsers in an automated way. In the past, developers had to perform manual steps to do this, including:

1. Opening up a browser
2. Pointing the browser to the project URL
3. Running the tests
4. Confirming that all tests have passed
5. Making changes
6. Refreshing the page

With Karma, automation gives the developer the ability to run a single command and determine whether an entire test suite has passed or failed. From a TDD perspective, this gives you the ability to find and fix failing tests quickly. Some of the pros and cons of using Karma compared to a manual process are as follows:

Pros	Cons
Ability to automate tests in multiple browsers and devices.	Additional tool to learn, configure, and maintain.
Ability to watch files.	
Online documentation and support.	
Does one thing—runs JavaScript tests—and does it well.	
Easy to integrate with a continuous integration server.	

Automating the process of testing and using Karma is extremely advantageous. In the TDD journey through this book, Karma will be one of your primary tools.

Protractor

Protractor is an end-to-end testing tool. It allows developers to mimic user interactions. It automates the testing of functionality and features through the interaction of a web browser. Protractor has specific methods to assist with testing AngularJS, but they are not exclusive to AngularJS. Some of the pros and cons of using Protractor are as follows:

Pros	Cons
Configurable to test multiple environments	Documentation and examples are limited
Easy integration with AngularJS	
Syntax and testing can be similar to the testing framework chosen for unit testing	

JavaScript testing frameworks

In this section, you will learn about the testing frameworks that will support you in your TDD practices. These include:

- Jasmine
- Selenium
- Mocha

Jasmine

Jasmine is a JavaScript testing framework. It can be easily integrated and run for websites and is agnostic to AngularJS. It provides spies and other features. It can also be run on its own without Karma. Some of the pros and cons are as follows:

Pros	Cons
Default integration with Karma.	No file-watching feature available when running tests. This means that tests have to be rerun by the user as they change.
Provides additional functions to assist with testing, such as test spies, fakes, and the pass-through functionality.	The learning curve can be steep for all the Protractor methods and features.
Cleans readable syntax that allows tests to be formatted in a way that relates to the behavior being tested.	
Integration with several output reporters.	

Selenium

Selenium (`http://www.seleniumhq.org/`) defines itself as:

> *"Selenium automates browsers. That's it!"*

Automation of browsers means that developers can interact with browsers easily. They can click on buttons or links, enter data, and so on. Selenium is a powerful toolset that, when used and set up properly, has lots of benefits; however, it can be confusing and cumbersome to set it up. Some of the pros and cons of Selenium are as follows:

Pros	Cons
Large feature set	Has to be run as a separate process
Distributed testing	Several steps to configure
SaaS support through services such as Sauce Labs	
Documentation and resources available	

As Protractor is a wrapper around Selenium, it won't be discussed in detail. Protractor will be further introduced in *Chapter 3, End-to-end Testing with Protractor*.

Mocha

Mocha is a testing framework originally written for Node.js applications but supports browser testing as well. It is very similar to Jasmine and mirrors much of its syntax. Let's discuss some of the pros and cons of Mocha:

Pros	Cons
Easy to install	Separate plugins/modules required for assertions, spies, and so on
Good documentation available	Additional configuration required to use it with Karma
Has several reporters	
Plugs in with several node projects	

The approach of being just a test runner and not worrying about assertions and mocking fits into the Node.js mantra—small individual modules that do one thing. For Node.js projects, I prefer to go with Mocha. The reason is that you can add new **Node Package Manager** (**npm**) modules for the specific plugins needed. When working with a website, and specifically AngularJS, I prefer to use Jasmine. It provides the features needed without having to install additional npm modules to a non-Node.js project.

Birth of Karma

When picking up a new tool, it is important to understand where it came from and why it was built. This section gives you some background of the origins of Karma.

The Karma difference

Karma was created by Vojtech Jína. The project was originally called testacular. In Vojtech Jína's thesis, he discusses the design, purpose, and implementation of Karma. In his thesis (*JavaScript Test Runner*, page 6, `https://github.com/karma-runner/karma/raw/master/thesis.pdf`), he describes Karma as:

> *"...a test runner, that helps web application developers to be more productive and effective by making automated testing simpler and faster. In fact, I have a much higher ambition and this thesis is only a part of it - I want to promote Test Driven Development (TDD) as "the" way to develop web applications, because I believe it is the most effective way to develop high quality software."*

Karma has the ability to easily and automatically run JavaScript unit tests on real browsers. Traditionally, tests were run by having to manually launch a browser and check for results by continually hitting the **Refresh** button. This method was awkward and often resulted in developers limiting the amount of tests that were written.

With Karma, a developer can write a test in almost any standard test framework, choose a browser to run against, set the files to watch for changes, and bam! Continuous automated testing. Simply check the output window for failed or passed tests.

Importance of combining Karma with AngularJS

Karma was built for AngularJS. Prior to Karma, there was a lack of automated testing tools for web-based JavaScript developers.

Remember, Karma is a test runner, not a test framework. Its job is to run tests and report which tests will pass or fail. Why is this helpful? A test framework is where you will write your tests. Apart from doing this, you will need to be focused on running the tests easily and seeing results. Karma easily runs tests across several different browsers. Karma also has some other features, such as file watching, which will be discussed further in detail later in the book.

Installing Karma

Time to start using Karma. Installations and applications are constantly changing. The following guide is intended to be brief in the hope that you will go to the Karma website, `http://karma-runner.github.io/`, and find the latest instructions.

The main focus of this section will be on the specific configuration used in this book and not an in-depth installation guide.

Installation prerequisites

To install Karma, you need to have Node.js on your computer. Node.js runs on Google's V8 engine and allows JavaScript to be run on several operating systems.

Developers can publish node applications and modules using npm. This allows developers to quickly integrate applications and modules into their applications.

Karma runs and is installed through the npm package, and therefore you need Node. js before you use or install Karma. To install Node.js, go to `http://nodejs.org/` and follow the installation instructions.

Assuming you have Node.js installed, type the following command in the command prompt to install Karma:

```
$ npm install karma -g
```

The preceding command uses npm to install Karma globally using `-g`. What this means is that you can use Karma on the command prompt by simply typing the following:

```
$ karma --version
```

By default, installing Karma will install `karma-chrome-launcher` and `karma-jasmine` as dependencies. Ensure that these modules are installed globally as well.

Configuring Karma

Karma comes equipped with an automated way to create a configuration file. To use the automated way, type the following command:

```
$ karma init
```

Here is a sample of the options chosen:

```
$ karma init

Which testing framework do you want to use ?
Press tab to list possible options. Enter to move to the next question.
> jasmine

Do you want to use Require.js ?
This will add Require.js plugin.
Press tab to list possible options. Enter to move to the next question.
> no

Do you want to capture a browser automatically ?
Press tab to list possible options. Enter empty string to move to the next question.
> Chrome
>

What is the location of your source and test files ?
You can use glob patterns, eg. "js/*.js" or "test/**/*Spec.js".
Enter empty string to move to the next question.
>

Should any of the files included by the previous patterns be excluded ?
You can use glob patterns, eg. "**/*.swp".
Enter empty string to move to the next question.
>

Do you want Karma to watch all the files and run the tests on change ?
Press tab to list possible options.
> yes
```

Customizing Karma's configuration

The following instructions describe the specific configuration required to get Karma running for the project. Customization includes the test framework (Jasmine), browser (Chrome) to test with, and files to test. To customize the configuration, open up `karma.conf` and perform the following steps:

1. Ensure that the enabled framework says `jasmine` using the following code:

   ```
   frameworks: ['jasmine'],
   ```

2. Configure the `test` directory. Note that the following definition needs to include the tests required to run along with any potential dependencies. The directory that will hold our tests is `/test/unit/`:

   ```
   files: [
   'test/unit/**/*.js'
   ],
   ```

3. Set the test browser to Chrome. It will then be initialized and will run a pop up after every test:

   ```
   browsers: ['Chrome'],
   ```

Confirming Karma's installation and configuration

To confirm Karma's installation and configuration, perform the following steps:

1. Run the following command to confirm that Karma starts with no errors:

   ```
   $ karma start
   ```

2. The output should be something like this:

   ```
   $ INFO [karma]: Karma v0.12.16 server started at
   http://localhost:9876/
   ```

3. In addition, the output should state that no test files were found:

   ```
   $ WARN [watcher]: Pattern "test/unit/**/*.js" does not match
   any file.
   ```

4. The output should do this along with a failed test message:

   ```
   $ Chrome 35.0.1916 (Windows 7): Executed 0 of 0 ERROR
   (0.016 secs / 0 secs)
   ```

This is expected as no tests have been created yet. Continue to the next step if Karma is started and you will see your Chrome browser with the following output:

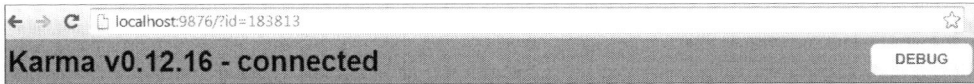

Common installation/configuration issues

If Jasmine or Chrome Launcher are missing, perform the following steps:

- When running the test, an error might occur saying `missing Jasmine or Chrome Launcher`. If you get this error, type the following command to install the missing dependencies:

```
$ npm install karma-jasmine -g
```

```
$ npm install karma-chrome-launcher -g
```

- Retry the test and confirm that the errors have been resolved.

The following is what you need to do to provide permissions (sudo/administrator):

- In some cases, you might not be able to install `npm_modules` globally using the `-g` command. This is generally due to permission issues on your computer. The resolution is to install Karma directly in your project folder. Use the same command without `-g` to do this:

```
$ npm install karma
```

- Run Karma using the relative path:

```
$ ./node_modules/karma/bin/karma --version
```

Now that Karma is installed and running, it's time to put it to use.

Testing with Karma

In this section, you will create a test to confirm Karma is working as expected. To do this, perform the following steps:

1. Create the test directory. In the Karma configuration, tests were defined in the following directory:

```
files: [
'test/unit/**/*.js'
],
```

Go ahead and create the `test/unit` directory.

2. Create a new file named `firstTest.js` in the `test/unit` directory.

3. Write the first test as follows:

```
describe('when testing karma', function (){
  it('should report a successful test', function (){
    expect(true).toBeTruthy();
  });
});
```

4. The preceding test uses Jasmine functions and has the following properties:

   ○ `describe`: This provides a brief string description of the things that will be tested

   ○ `it`: This provides a brief string of the specific assertion

   ○ `expect`: This provides a way to assert values

   ○ `toBeTruthy`: This is one of several properties on an expectation that can be used to make assertions

   This test has no real value other than to confirm the output of a passing test.

5. Bam! Check your console window and see that Karma has executed your test. Your command line should say something like this:

```
$ INFO [watcher]: Added file "./test/unit/firstTest.js"
```

This output means that Karma automagically recognized that a new file was added. The next output should say something like this:

```
$ Chrome 35.0.1916 (Windows 7): Executed 1 of 1 SUCCESS
(0.02 secs / 0.015 secs)
```

This means your test has passed!

Confirming the Karma installation

Now the initial set up and configuration of Karma is complete. Here is a review of the steps:

- Installed Karma through the npm command
- Initialized a default configuration through the `karma init` command
- Configured Karma with Jasmine and a `test/unit` test directory
- Started Karma and confirmed it could be opened with Chrome
- Added a Jasmine test, `firstTest.js`, to our `test/unit` test directory
- Karma recognized that `firstTest.js` had been added to the test directory
- Karma executed our `firstTest.js` and reported our output

With a couple of steps, you were able to see Karma running and executing tests automatically. From a TDD perspective, you can focus on moving tests from failing to passing without much effort. No need to refresh the browser; just check the command output window. Keep Karma running and all your tests and files will automatically be added and run.

In the next sections, you will see how to apply Karma with a TDD approach. If you're OK with Karma so far and want to move on to Protractor, continue to the next chapter.

Using Karma with AngularJS

Here, you will walk through a TDD approach to an AngularJS component. By the end of this chapter, you should be able to:

- Feel confident about using Karma and its configuration
- Understand the basic components of a Jasmine test
- Start to understand how to integrate a TDD approach in an AngularJS application

Getting AngularJS

An easy method for installing AngularJS into projects is to use Bower. Feel free to install AngularJS into your project in any way you prefer. Following is a brief description on how to install and use Bower.

Bower

Bower is a package manager for JavaScript components. Bower allows client-side JavaScript components to be versioned and automatically downloaded into your projects. This allows you to upgrade third-party tools and components and provide an easy, standard way to use tools such as AngularJS, Bootstrap, and many more.

Bower installation

Bower is an npm module, just like Karma. Ensure you have Node.js installed before you try to install Bower using the following steps:

1. Ensure you have Bower installed using this code:

```
$ npm install bower -g
```

2. Initialize the `bower.json` configuration in the root of the project:

```
$ bower init
```

```
//This will create a bower.json file which contains the dependent
packages
```

```
//Answer default to all the questions.
```

The output should be something like what is shown in the following screenshot:

That is it. Now Bower is installed and ready to download JavaScript packages into your project.

Installing AngularJS

Use the following command to install AngularJS using Bower:

```
$ bower install angular
```

Type the previous command in your command prompt for the directory you will be working in. After the installation is complete, look at your directory and confirm that a `bower_componets` directory was created. Inside this, there should be a folder for AngularJS:

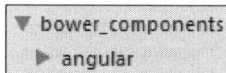

Installing Angular mocks

Angular mocks allows you to test AngularJS components. The official definition, which is found at `https://docs.angularjs.org/api/ngMock`, is as follows:

> *"The ngMock module provides support to inject and mock Angular services into unit tests. In addition, ngMock also extends various core ng services such that they can be inspected and controlled in a synchronous manner within test code."*

To install Angular mocks, simply use Bower:

```
$ bower install angular-mocks
```

Initializing Karma

A `karma.conf` file is required to tell Karma how it should run for the application in question. The best way to initialize it is to run the following command in the command prompt:

```
$ karma init
```

Use the default answers. After `karma.conf` has been created in the current directory, open up the configuration. The one configuration that needs to change is the definition of the files for Karma to use. Use the following definition in the `files` section, which defines the files required to run the test:

```
files: [
    'bower_components/angular/angular.js',
    'bower_components/angular-mocks/angular-mocks.js',
    'app/**/*.js',
    'spec/**/*.js'
],
```

The preceding configuration loads `angular.js`, JavaScript files in the `app` directory, and your tests in the `spec` folder.

Ensure that Karma can run your configuration:

```
$ karma start
```

The command output should state something like this:

```
$ Chrome 35.0.1916 (Windows 7): Executed 0 of 0 ERROR
(0.01 secs / 0 secs)
```

That is it. Karma is now running for the first AngularJS application.

Testing with AngularJS and Karma

The purpose of this first test using Karma is to create a dynamic to-do list. This walk through will follow the TDD steps we discussed in *Chapter 1, Introduction to Test-driven Development*: test first, make it run, and make it better. This will allow you to gain more experience in using TDD with AngularJS.

A development to-do list

Before you start the test, set your focus on what needs to be developed using a development to-do list. This will allow you to organize your thoughts. Here is the to-do list:

- Maintain a list of items:
  - The example list consists of test, execute, and refactor

- Add an item to the list:
  - The example list after you add the item is test, execute, refactor, and repeat

- Remove an item from the list:
  - The example list after you add and remove the item is test, execute, and refactor

Testing a list of items

The first development item is to provide you with the ability to have a list of items on a controller. The next couple of steps will walk you through the TDD process of adding the first feature using the TDD life cycle that is test first, make it run, make it better.

Test first

Determining where to start is often the hardest part. The best way is to remember the 3 A's (Assemble, Act, and Assert) and start with the base Jasmine template format. The code to do this is as follows:

```
describe('',function(){

beforeEach(function(){
  });
```

```
it('',function(){
});
});
```

- `describe`: This defines the main feature we are testing. The string will explain the feature in readable terms and then the function will follow with the test.

- `beforeEach`: This is the assemble step. The function defined in `beforeEach` will get executed before every assert. It is best to put the test setup required before each test in this function.

- `it`: This is the act and assert step. In the `it` section, you will perform the action being tested, followed by some assertion. The act step doesn't have to go into the `it` function. Depending on the test, it might be more suited in the `beforeEach` function.

Assemble, Act, and Assert (3 A's)

Now that the template is there, we can start filling in the pieces. We will again follow the 3 A's mantra.

The following are the two parts of the assemble section.

In the first part, we initialize the module using the following code:

```
...
beforeEach(function(){
  module('todo');
});
...
```

This code will use the Angular mocks JavaScript library to initialize the AngularJS module being tested. We haven't defined the `todo` module, but we will do this after we get a failing test.

The second part talks about the scope of `TodoController`. The `TodoController` scope will contain the list of items on its `scope` variable. It is required that the test has access to the scope of `TodoController`. Angular mocks will be used to get this. Add the following code to `beforeEach` to get the controller's scope:

```
// scope -hold items on the controller
var scope = {};

beforeEach(function(){
//...
```

```
//inject - access angular controllerinject(function($controller){
    //$controller - initialize controller with test scope
    $controller('TodoController',{$scope:scope});
});
//...
});
```

The following is a brief explanation of each of the code elements:

- `scope`: This variable is used to hold and test the list items on the controller.
- `inject`: The Angular mocks function is used to access AngularJS's `$controller`. This essentially allows you to get access and inject dependencies into AngularJS objects.
- `$controller`: This initializes the scope of `TodoController`. The test's `scope` variable will now contain the controller's scope.

In the case of "act", there is no method to act on. The `scope` object has already been retrieved as part of the assemble step.

In assert, there are two parts again:

- The first assertion is to ensure the `TodoController` scope has a `list` variable defined with three items. The `list` variable will be used to hold the list of all the items:

    ```
    it('should define a list object',function(){
    expect(scope.list).toBeDefined();
    });
    ```

- The second, third, and fourth assertions will be used to confirm whether the data in the list is in the correct order, that is, first is test, second is execute, and third is refactor:

    ```
    //Second test
    it('should define a list object', function(){
    expect(scope.list[0]).toEqual('test');
    });
    //Third test
    it('should define a list object', function(){
    expect(scope.list[1]).toEqual('execute');
    });
    //Fourth test
    it('should define a list object', function(){
    expect(scope.list[2]).toEqual('refactor');
    });
    ```

Make it run

The next step in the TDD life cycle is to make the application run and fix the code so that the tests pass. Remember, think about the smallest components that can be added to make the test pass by proceeding with the following steps:

1. Run Karma by typing the following command:

    ```
    $ karma start
    ```

2. If you encounter `[$injector:moduler] Failed to instantiate module todo due to error`, then it can be due to the following:

    ○   The preceding error message is saying that the `todo` module hasn't been defined. Since the error message is telling you what is required, this is the perfect place to start. Create a new file in the app directory named `todo`. The working directory should now look something like this:

    ```
    ▼ app
        todo.js
    ▶ bower_components
    ▼ spec
        todo.js
      karma.conf.js
    ```

    ○   Add the `todo` module to the beginning of your new file as follows:

    ```
    angular.module('todo',[]);
    ```

    ○   Review the console window where Karma is running. You should now see a new error.

3. Error: The `[ng:areq] argument TodoController is not a function, got undefined`:

    ○   This error message is describing exactly what needs to be done. There is no need to decipher error messages or stack traces. Simply update the `todo.js` file so it contains an AngularJS controller as follows:

    ```
    angular.module('todo',[])
    .controller('TodoController',[])
    ```

    ○   In the previous code, we didn't try and define the logic required; we only added the smallest component to meet the error message. Review the console window for the next error.

4. Error: `The expected undefined to be defined as follows:`

   ○ The new error message is again clear. We can also see that the code has now passed up to the point of our assertion at the following point:

   ```
   expect(scope.list).toBeDefined();
   ```

   ○ As there is no list on the scope, you need to add one. Update the `app/todo.js` file as follows:

   ```
   .controller('TodoController',['$scope',function($scope){
   $scope.list = [];
   }])
   ```

   ○ Review the console window.

5. You should now see one of the four tests pass! This means you have successfully used TDD and Karma to get your first test to pass. Now you need to fix the other three. The next error is `Expected undefined to equal 'test'`:

   ○ The error output again describes exactly what needs to happen. You just need to initialize the array with the elements test, execute, and run. Go to `app/todo.js` and add the data to the array initialization:

   ```
   angular.module('todo',[])
   .controller('TodoController',['$scope',function($scope){
   $scope.list = ['test','execute','refactor'];
   }]);
   ```

   ○ Review the output in the Karma window.

6. Excellent! The output is in green and states that all the tests have passed.

   The result module and controller code from this step is as follows:

   ```
   //A module for the application
   angular.module('todo',[])
     //A controller to manage the to-do items.controller(
     'TodoController',['$scope', function($scope){
   //the initialization of items on the controller scope
   $scope.list = ['test','execute','refactor'];
   }]);
   ```

Now that the "make it run" step is complete, you can move on to the next step and make it better.

Make it better

Until this point, there was nothing required to directly refactor or that had been identified in the development to-do list. A review of the development to-do list shows that an item can be crossed out:

- View a list of to-do list items:
  - The example list consists of test, execute, and refactor
- Add an item to a to-do-list:
  - The example list after you add the item will consist of test, execute, refactor, and repeat
- Remove an item from a to-do-list:
  - The example list after you add and then remove the item will consist of test, execute, and refactor

Next up is the requirement to add a new item to the list. The TDD rhythm will be followed again: test first, make it run, and make it better.

Adding a function to the controller

The next task is to give the controller the ability to add items to the scope list. This will require the addition of a method to the scope. This walk-through will follow the same TDD steps as done previously.

Test first

Instead of creating a new file and duplicating some of the assemble steps, the following test will be inserted under the last `it` method. The reason is because the same module and controller will be used:

```
describe('when using a to-do list', function(){
  var scope = null;
  beforeEach(function(){
  //...
  });
  //...

  describe('',function(){

    beforeEach(function(){
    });

    it('',function(){
```

```
    });
  });
});
```

Assemble, Act, and Assert (3 A's)

Now that the template is there, we can start filling in the gaps using the 3 A's mantra:

1. **Assemble**: There is no initialization or setup required, as the module and controller scope will be inherited.

2. **Act**: Here, you need to act on the add method with a new item. We place the act function into the before each function. This allows us to repeat the same step if/when more tests are added:

   ```
   beforeEach(function(){
   scope.add('repeat');
   });
   ```

3. **Assert**: Here, an item should be added to the list, and then you need to confirm that the last item in the array is as expected:

   ```
   it('should add item to last item in list',function(){
   var lastIndexOfList = scope.list.length - 1;
   expect(scope.list[lastIndexOfList]).toEqual('repeat');
   });
   ```

Make it run

The next step in the TDD life cycle is to make it run. Remember, think about the smallest components that can be added to make the test pass, as follows:

1. Ensure Karma is running in your console by typing in the following command:

   ```
   $ karma start
   ```

2. The first error will state TypeError: undefined is not a function:

   ◦ The error refers to the following line of code:

     ```
     scope.add('repeat');
     ```

   ◦ The error is telling you that the add method hasn't been defined. The add function will need to be added to the app/todo.js code. The controller has already been defined, so the add function needs to be placed on the controller's scope:

     ```
     angular.module('to-do', [])
     .controller('TodoController', ['$scope', function($scope) {
     ```

```
//...
$scope.add = function(){};
}]);
```

- ○ Notice how the add function doesn't contain any logic. The smallest component has been added to get the test to satisfy the error message.

- ○ Review the console window for the next error.

3. Error: `Expected 'refactor' to equal 'repeat'`:

- ○ Have a look at the following expectation:

```
it('should add item to last item in list',function(){
    var lastIndexOfList = scope.list.length - 1;
    expect(scope.list[lastIndexOfList]).toEqual('repeat');
});
```

- ○ The failed assertion in step 2 is telling us that based on the preceding expectation, the expected result of repeat is not what the last item in the list has. The smallest possible thing that can be added to make this assertion pass is to push repeat to the end of the list in the add function. Here is how to do this:

```
//...
$scope.add = function(){
    $scope.list.push('repeat');
};
//...
```

- ○ Review the console to see what the next output says.

4. Success! All five tests have now passed.

The resulting code added to get the tests to pass is as follows:

```
//A module for the application
angular.module('todo',[])
  //A controller to manage the to-do items
.controller('TodoController',['$scope', function($scope){
    //the initialization of items on the controller scope
    $scope.list = ['test','execute','refactor'];

    $scope.add = function(){
        $scope.list.push('repeat');
    };
}]);
```

Make it better

The main thing that we need to refactor is that the add function still hasn't been fully implemented. It contains a hardcoded value, and the minute we send in a different item into the add function, the test will fail.

Keep Karma running so we can keep passing the tests as changes are made. The main issue with the current add method is as follows:

* It doesn't accept any parameter
* It doesn't push a parameter onto the list but uses a hardcoded value

The resultant add function should now look as follows:

```
$scope.add = function(item){
  $scope.list.push(item);
};
```

Confirm that the Karma output still displays success:

```
$ Chrome 35.0.1916 (Windows 7): Executed 5 of 5 SUCCESS (0.165 secs /
0.153 secs)
```

Self-test questions

Self-test questions will help you further test your knowledge of using TDD with AngularJS and Karma.

Q1. How do you use Karma to create a configuration file?

1. `karma config`
2. `karma init`
3. `karma -config karma.conf.js`

Q2. The Jasmine test method named `before` gets executed before every test.

1. True
2. False

Q3. Bower is used to install Karma.

1. True
2. False

Q4. The 3 A's stand for which one of these?

1. A group of super heroes
2. Assemble, Act, and Assert
3. Accept, approve, and act

Summary

In this chapter, we reviewed JavaScript testing frameworks and tools and discussed how Vojtech Jína created Karma. We saw how to install, configure, and run Karma. Finally, you have walked through an example of using Karma with TDD. In the next chapter, you will learn about end-to-end testing with Protractor.

3
End-to-end Testing
with Protractor

Unit testing is only one aspect of testing. In this chapter, we will look at end-to-end testing applications, through all layers of an application. You will be introduced to Protractor, the end-to-end testing tool from the AngularJS team. We will look into why it was created and the problems it solves. Finally, we will see how to install, configure, and use Protractor with TDD.

An overview of Protractor

Protractor is an end-to-end testing tool that runs using Node.js and is available as an npm package. Before talking about Protractor specifically, you need to understand what end-to-end testing is. End-to-end testing is testing an application against all the interconnected moving parts and layers of an application. This differs from unit tests, where the focus is on individual components such as controllers, services, directives, and so on. With end-to-end testing, the focus is on how the application or a module, as a whole, works, such as confirming the click of a button does x, y, and z.

Protractor allows the end-to-end testing of an application. This includes the ability to simulate the click of a button and interact with an application in the same way a user would. It then allows expectations to be set based on what the user would expect. To put this into context, think about the following user specification:

Assuming I input abc into the search box, the following should occur:

- The search button is hit
- At least one result should be received

The preceding specification describes a basic search feature. Nothing in the preceding specification describes a controller, directive, or service; it only describes the expected application behavior. If a user were to test the specification, they may perform the following steps:

1. Point the browser to the website
2. Select the input field
3. Type abc in the input field
4. Click on the **Search** button
5. Confirm that the search output displays at least one result.

The structure and syntax of Protractor mirrors that of Jasmine and the tests you wrote in *Chapter 2, The Karma Way*. You can think of Protractor as a wrapper around Jasmine, with added features to support end-to-end testing. To write an end-to-end test with Protractor, we can follow the same steps as described in the preceding steps, but with code. Here are the steps in code:

1. Point the browser to the website:

   ```
   browser.get('/');
   ```

2. Select the input field:

   ```
   var inputField = element.all(by.css('input'));
   ```

3. Type abc in the input field:

   ```
   inputField.setText('abc');
   ```

4. Click on the **Search** button:

   ```
   inputField.click();
   ```

5. Find the search result details on the page:

   ```
   var searchResults = element.all(by.css('#searchResult'));
   ```

6. Finally, the assertion needs to be made that at least one or more search results are available on the screen:

   ```
   expect(searchResults).count() >= 1);
   ```

As a complete test, the code will be as follows:

```
describe('Given I input 'abc' into the search box',function(){
  //1 - Point browser to website
  browser.get('/');
  //2 - Select input field
```

```
var inputField = element.all(by.css('input'));
//3 - Type abc into input field
inputField.setText('abc');
//4 - Push search button
inputField.click();

it('should display search results',function(){
    // 5 - Find the search result details
    var searchResults = element.all(by.css('#searchResult'));
    //6 - Assert
    expect(searchResults).count() >= 1);
  });
});
```

That's it! When Protractor runs, it will open a browser, go to the website, follow the instructions, and finally check the expectations. The trick with end-to-end testing is having a clear vision on what the user specification is, and then translating that specification to code.

The previous example is a high-level view of what will be described throughout this chapter. Now that you have been introduced to Protractor, the rest of the chapter will show how Protractor works behind the scenes, how to install it, and finally, walk you through a complete example using TDD.

Origins of Protractor

Protractor is not the first end-to-end testing tool that the AngularJS team built. The first tool was called **Scenario Runner**. In order to understand why Protractor was built, we need to first look at its predecessor: Scenario Runner.

End of life

Scenario Runner is in maintenance mode and has reached its end of life. It has been deprecated in place of Protractor. In this section, we will look at what Scenario Runner was and what gaps the tool had.

The birth of Protractor

Julie Ralph is the primary contributor to Protractor. According to Julie Ralph, the motivation for Protractor was based on the following experience with Angular Scenario Runner, on another project within Google (`http://javascriptjabber.com/106-jsj-protractor-with-julie-ralph/`):

> *We tried using the Scenario Runner. And we found that it really just couldn't do the things that we needed to test. We needed to test things like logging in. And your login page isn't an Angular page. And the Scenario Runner couldn't deal with that. And it couldn't deal with things like popups and multiple windows, navigating the browser history, stuff like that.*

Based on her experience with Scenario Runner, Julie Ralph decided to create Protractor to fill the gaps.

Protractor takes advantage of the maturity of the Selenium project, and wraps up its methods so that it can be easily used for AngularJS projects. Remember, Protractor is about testing through the eyes of the user. It was designed to test all layers of an application: Web UI, backend services, persistence layer, and so on.

Life without Protractor

Unit testing is not the only testing that needs to be written and maintained. Unit tests focus on small individual components of an application. By testing small components, the confidence in the code and logic grows. Unit tests don't focus on how the complete system works when interconnected.

End-to-end testing with Protractor allows the developer to focus on the complete behavior of a feature or module. Going back to the search example, the test should only pass if the whole user specification passes; enter data into the search box, click on the **Search** button, and see the results.

Protractor is not the only end-to-end testing framework out there, but it is the best choice for AngularJS applications. Here are a few reasons why you should choose Protractor:

- It is documented throughout the AngularJS tutorials and examples.
- It can be written using multiple JavaScript testing frameworks, including Jasmine and Mocha.
- It provides convenience methods for AngularJS components, including waiting for a page to load, expectations on promises, and so on.
- It wraps Selenium methods that automatically wait for promises to be fulfilled.

- It is supported by **SaaS (Software as a Service)** providers such as Sauce Labs, which is available at `https://saucelabs.com/`.

- It is supported and maintained by the same company that maintains AngularJS and Google.

Protractor installation

It's time to start getting our hands dirty, and install and configure Protractor. Installations and applications are constantly changing. The main focus will be on the specific configuration used in this book, and not an in-depth installation guide. There are several varying different configurations, so please review the Protractor site for additional details. Please visit the following website to find the latest installation and configuration guide:

`http://angular.github.io/protractor/`

For this book, we will only be using the `chromeOnly` configuration. The `chromeOnly` configuration doesn't require several moving parts, and allows you to get up to speed quickly. As your tests grow and you are required to support multiple browsers, running tests with a Selenium server or using something like Sauce Labs should be reviewed. *Appendix A, Integrating Selenium Server with Protractor* describes how to set up a standalone Selenium server.

Installation prerequisites

Protractor has the following prerequisites:

- **Node.js**: Protractor is a Node.js module available using npm. The best way to install Node.js is to follow the instructions on the official site at `http://nodejs.org/download/`.

- **Chrome**: This is a web browser built by Google. It will be used to run end-to-end tests in Protractor without the need for a Selenium server. Follow the installation instructions on the official site at `http://www.google.com/chrome/browser/`.

- **Selenium WebDriver for Chrome**: This is a tool that allows you to interact with web applications. Selenium WebDriver is provided with the Protractor npm module. We will walk through the instructions as we install Protractor.

Installing Protractor

Here are the steps to install Protractor:

1. Once Node.js is installed and available in the command prompt, type the following command to install Protractor in the current directory:

    ```
    $ npm install protractor
    ```

    The previous command uses Node's npm command to install Protractor in the current local directory.

2. Confirm the current directory structure:

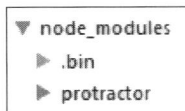

    ```
    ▼ node_modules
      ▶ .bin
      ▶ protractor
    ```

    To use Protractor in the command prompt, use the relative path to the Protractor bin directory.

3. Test that the Protractor version can be determined as follows:

    ```
    $ ./node_modules/protractor/bin/protractor --version
    ```

Installing WebDriver for Chrome

Here are the steps to install WebDriver for Chrome:

1. To install Selenium WebDriver for Chrome, go to the webdriver-manager executable in the Protractor bin directory that can be found at ./node_modules/protractor/bin/ and type the following:

    ```
    $ ./node_modules/protractor/bin/webdriver-manager update
    ```

2. Confirm the directory structure.

    The previous command will create a Selenium directory containing the required Chrome driver used in the project. The node_modules directory should now look like the following:

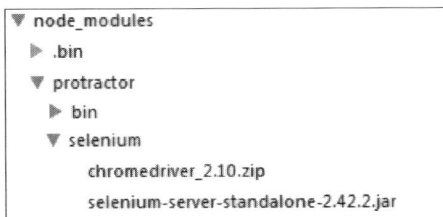

    ```
    ▼ node_modules
      ▶ .bin
      ▼ protractor
        ▶ bin
        ▼ selenium
            chromedriver_2.10.zip
            selenium-server-standalone-2.42.2.jar
    ```

The installation is now complete. Both Protractor and Selenium WebDriver for Chrome have been installed. We can now move on to the configuration.

Customizing configuration

In this section, we will be configuring Protractor using the following steps:

1. Start with a standard template configuration.

   Fortunately, the Protractor installation comes with some base configurations in its installation directory. Going back to the local `node_modules` directory, you should find the example Chrome configuration in the example folder:

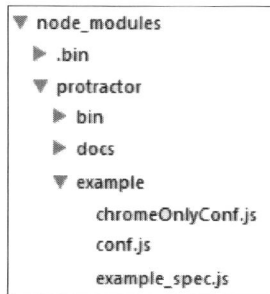

   ```
   ▼ node_modules
      ▶ .bin
      ▼ protractor
         ▶ bin
         ▶ docs
         ▼ example
            chromeOnlyConf.js
            conf.js
            example_spec.js
   ```

   The example directory contains example configurations. The one that we will use is called `chromeOnlyConf.js`. The `chromeOnly` configuration will allow us to run end-to-end tests in Chrome without the need for a Selenium server. As discussed earlier, running a Selenium server is another option that will not be discussed in this book.

2. Review the example configuration file:

   ○ The `chromeOnly` parameter should be set to `true`, as follows:

   ```
   exports.config = {
   //...
     chromeOnly: true,
     //...
   };
   ```

   ○ The `chromeDriver` parameter will have to be modified to point to the driver we installed, as follows:

   ```
   exports.config = {
   //...
     chromeDriver: '../selenium/chromedriver',
     //...
   };
   ```

○ The `capabilities` parameter should only specify the name of the browser:

```
exports.config = {
//...
  capabilities: {
'browserName': 'chrome'
},
//...
};
```

○ The final important configuration is the source file declaration:

```
exports.config = {
  //...
  specs: ['example_spec.js'],
  //...
};
```

Excellent! Now we have Protractor installed and configured.

Confirming installation and configuration

To confirm installation, Protractor requires at least one file defined in the `specs` configuration section. Before adding a real test and complicating things, create an empty file in the root directory called `confirmConfigTest.js`. Then, add the test to the `specs` section so it looks like this:

```
    specs: ['confirmConfigTest.js'],
```

To confirm that Protractor has been installed, run Protractor by going to the root of your project directory and type:

```
$ ./node_modules/protractor/bin/protractor chromeOnlyConf.js
```

If everything was set up correctly and installed, you should see something similar to this in your command prompt:

```
Finished in 0.0002 seconds

0 tests, 0 assertions, 0 failures
```

Common installation/configuration issues

The following are some common issues that you might come across while installing WebDriver for Chrome:

- `Selenium not installed correctly`: If the tests have errors related to the Selenium WebDriver location, you need to ensure that you followed the steps to update WebDriver. The update step downloads the WebDriver components into the local Protractor installation folder. Until WebDriver has been updated, you won't be able to reference it in the Protractor configuration. An easy way to confirm the update is to look in the Protractor directory and ensure that a Selenium folder exists.

- `Unable to find tests`: When no tests are executed by Protractor, it can be frustrating. The best place to start is in the configuration file. Make sure the relative path and any file names or extensions are correct.

For a more complete list, please refer to the official Protractor site at `http://angular.github.io/protractor/`.

Hello Protractor

With the Protractor installation and configuration complete, you can look at writing a real test. This section will walk you through using TDD with Protractor. At the end of this chapter, you should be able to:

- Feel confident in using and configuring Protractor
- Understand the basic components of a Protractor test
- Start to understand how to integrate a TDD approach to end-to-end testing

TDD end-to-end

Test-driven development is not a silver bullet. It is a foundation of principles and techniques used to improve efficiency, quality, and much more. Knowing how to apply TDD is the first step, but knowing when to apply it is just as important.

When applying TDD, you are coupling tests to your logic and code. As a developer, you have to make decisions on when that coupling makes sense and will be advantageous to your project. As you work through the examples, be aware that they show you how to apply TDD techniques. As you use these practices in your own projects, you will need to determine the depth and coupling of the tests that your project and specifications require.

The pre-setup

The code in this test will leverage the unit tested code from *Chapter 2, The Karma Way*. You will need to copy the code to a new directory.

As a reminder, the application was a to-do application that adds and deletes items from a list. It has a single controller, `TodoController`, that has a list of items and an `add` method. The application didn't have any HTML or user components. We will use a TDD approach to add the UI elements. The current code directory should be structured as follows:

```
▼ todo
    ▼ app
        todo.js
    ▶ bower_components
    ▶ spec
      karma.conf
```

The setup

The setup will mirror the installation and configuration steps from earlier:

1. Install Protractor.
2. Update Selenium WebDriver.
3. Configure Protractor based on the example configuration.

Follow the Protractor installation and configuration steps you learned in the previous section in a new project directory. The only difference is that the Protractor tests should be placed in a `spec/e2e` directory. This will allow you to easily identify the tests in your project structure. After creating a `spec/e2e` directory update, the Protractor configuration `spec` section should be as follows:

```
exports.config = {
  //...
  specs: ['spec/e2e/**/*.js'],
  //...
};
```

After confirming that Protractor has been installed and configured properly, you can start the first test.

Test first

Now that Protractor has been set up, the testing can begin. End-to-end tests are slow and touch multiple layers of the application. They also require the full application to be set up and running in order to test. There are several techniques that we can leverage to mock a local environment. Mocking data and APIs will be discussed in *Chapter 7, Give Me Some Data*. This first end-to-end test will only have a Web UI layer. No additional mocking will be required.

As mentioned earlier, Protractor requires a running application. This means the website needs to be available for you to point your browser to it. A simple approach to serving static HTTP content is to use the `http-server` npm module. The `http-server` module is perfect for a local development environment, but probably not suited for the final application infrastructure. Your production website might be developed in something like Express, IIS, or Apache.

Installing the test web server

To install our test web server, we will use the `http-server` node module. The advantage of a web server such as `http-server` is that it requires very little configuration and can just start and run the website. Here are the steps to install the web server:

1. Type the following command in the command line:

   ```
   $ npm install http-server
   ```

2. Now create a stub `index.html` page at the root of the project with the basic HTML components:

   ```
   <!DOCTYPE html>
   <html>
   <head>
     <title></title>
   </head>
   <body>

   </body>
   </html>
   ```

3. Now run the HTTP server and ensure the page is loaded:

   ```
   ./node_modules/http-server/bin/http-server -p 8080
   ```

4. Go to `http://localhost:8080`. You should see a blank page get loaded, with no errors in the command or on the web page. If you see errors, ensure that the directory has the required `index.html` file. Now that you have a working website, it is time to configure Protractor to use it.

Configuring Protractor

Protractor can be configured with a base URL for an application. By specifying a base URL, tests will look cleaner and can be easily configured to use different URLs for the same application. Imagine a dev, qa, and production URL that use the same tests, but have different URLs that need to be tested.

As we will be running this locally, we will need to use `http://localhost:8000` as our base URL. Update the Protractor configuration file as follows:

```
baseUrl: 'http://localhost:8080/'
```

Getting down to business

End-to-end testing is different than unit testing. Tests will interact with different layers of an application throughout a single scenario. You may have another team designing the HTML elements, CSS, and so on. The development team will then have to integrate the UI HTML into the page. The TDD approach will allow you to create tests for separate components independently. The idea is you want to be able test the features of the application that make sense to test. Testing everything blindly can be a waste of time and a refactoring nightmare.

In this case, we start with a blank canvas of a page and want to test the behavior of the primary components. We will follow the TDD life cycle (test, execute, refactor). In the upcoming sections, we will cover the following steps:

1. Review the user specification.
2. Write down the main tasks that need to be developed.
3. Write the test for what will be developed.

Specification

The purpose of this first test is to manage a dynamic to-do list.

The development to-do list

We will need a development to-do list to set our focus and organize our development tasks. Perform the following steps:

1. View the to-do list items

   ◦ **Example list**: test, execute, refactor

2. Add an item to the to-do list

   ◦ **Example list**: test, execute, refactor, repeat

3. Remove an item from the to-do list

   ◦ **Example list**: test, execute, refactor

If you recall, in our previous example, we set up the backend module for the to-do list application. In this case, we will focus on managing the list from the user's perspective.

Test first

Just as we discussed with the Karma test, start with the 3 A's (Assemble, Act, Assert). Protractor tests are written in the same Jasmine style and setup, so you don't have to learn any new syntax. Start with the basic Jasmine template format:

```
describe('',function(){
  beforeEach(function(){
  });
  it('',function(){
  });
});
```

- `describe`: This defines the main feature we test. The first parameter is a string to explain the feature and the second parameter is the function that contains the test steps.

- `beforeEach`: This is the test setup and Assemble section. The function defined in `beforeEach` will be executed before every Assert. This is where we perform any setup mocks, spies, and other components needed to test.

- `it`: This is the Act and Assert section. In this section, you will perform the actual action being tested, followed by an assertion.

Assemble, Act, Assert (3 A's)

Follow the 3 A's mantra:

- **Assemble**: As this is an end-to-end test, we will initialize by directing the test to go to the page under test. In this case, the page is /. This is because we set the base URL to be `http://localhost:8080/` in the configuration file. So the code will look like the following:

```
beforeEach(function(){
  browser.get('/');
});
```

- **Act**: In the first test, to view a list of to-do items, there is no button to be clicked or action to be done in order to get the list. We should just browse to the page and see the list of to-do items.

- **Assert**: This is our first failing test, which we will write using Protractor. The test needs to determine whether the list of to-do items, that is test, execute, and refactor, is available on the page. In AngularJS, this will be done using `ng-repeat`, meaning each item in a list will be repeated with some special HTML to display an individual item.

  As Protractor is testing the actual UI, you will need to have the ability to select HTML elements. One of the benefits of Protractor is that it wraps up AngularJS components so that they can be easily tested.

  In the preceding test, we will use the `element` selector with the `by.repeater` selection. In our case, the first assertion will look like this:

```
it('',function(){
  var todoListItems = element.all(by.repeater('item in list'));
  expect(todoListItems.count()).toBe(3);
});
```

  The first line will select the to-do list items available on the page. The second will Assert that the item count is 3. When running the test, ensure the web server is still running using the following command:

```
$./node_modules/http-server/bin/http-server -p 8080
```

The completed test looks as follows:

```
describe('',function(){
  //ASSEMBLE
  beforeEach(function(){
    //ACT
    browser.get('/');
  });
```

```
it('',function(){
  var todoListItems = element.all(by.repeater('item in list'));
  //ASSERT
  expect(todoListItems.count()).toBe(3);
});
});
```

Running the test

The steps to run a test are as follows:

1. Run the Protractor test in a different command prompt, using the following command:

   ```
   $ protractor chromeOnlyConf.js
   ```

2. The output should say that AngularJS could not be found:

   ```
   $ Error: Angular could not be found on the page
   http://localhost:8080/ : retries looking for angular exceeded
   ```

   This error indicates that the assertions failed.

3. When running the test, you should see a Chrome pop-up with the page. You should also see that the output from the web server says something like the following:

   GET /" "Mozilla/5.0 (Windows NT 6.1; WOW64) AppleWebKit/537.36 (KHTML, like Gecko) Chrome/36.0.1985.125 Safari/537.36

Excellent! Now you've got a failing Protractor test, it is time to make it run.

Make it run

The next step in the TDD life cycle is to execute and fix the code so that the tests pass. As you walk through the test, remember to use the smallest components that can be added to make the test pass:

1. As the first error says, `Angular can't be found`. Add AngularJS to the page just before the closing tag for the body as follows:

   ```
   //...
     <script src="bower_components/angular/angular.js"></script>
   </body>
   //...
   ```

2. Rerun the test using the following command:

```
$ protractor chromeOnlyConf.js
```

The output should now display the following:

```
$ Error: Angular could not be found on the page
http://localhost:8080/ : angular never provided resume
Bootstrap
```

3. Since you haven't specified the application or added the `todo.js` page, let's add these components to it after the AngularJS script:

```
//...
<body ng-app="todo">
  <script
src="bower_components/angular/angular.js"></script>
  <script src="app/todo.js"></script>
//...
```

4. Rerun the test using the following command:

```
$ protractor chromeOnlyConf.js
```

The output should now display that our expectations failed:

```
$ Expected 0 to be 3.
```

Great! Now there are no more execution errors in our page, only the failed expectations on the number of list items.

5. In order to add the items to the page, we will need to add a reference to `TodoController`, and then add `ng-repeat` for each item. The code in the `index.html` page should be as follows:

```
<div ng-controller="TodoController">
  <ul ng-repeat="item in list">
    <li>{{item}}</li>
  </ul>
</div>
```

6. Rerun the test as follows:

```
$ protractor chromeOnlyConf.js
```

The output should now display that our assertion and test passed:

```
$ 1 test, 1 assertion, 0 failures
```

The completed page body tag will now look as follows:

```
<body ng-app="todo">
<div ng-controller="TodoController">
  <ul ng-repeat="item in list">
    <li>{{item}}</li>
  </ul>
</div>

  <script src="bower_components/angular/angular.js"></script>
  <script src="app/todo.js"></script>
</body>
```

Make it better

There is nothing that was called out to refactor. Looking at our to-do list, we tackled the first two items from an end-to-end perspective.

1. View the to-do-list items:
   ° **Example list**: test, execute, refactor
2. Add an item to a to-do-list:
   ° **Example list**: test, execute, refactor, repeat
3. Remove an item from a to-do-list:
   ° **Example list**: test, execute, refactor

I will leave the second and third items as an exercise, so that you can further explore and practice TDD with Protractor.

Cleaning up the gaps

There are a couple of things that were discussed in this chapter that need some further clarification. This includes the following:

- Where is the asynchronous logic?
- How to really implement TDD with end-to-end tests.

Async magic

In the preceding tests, we saw some magic that you might be questioning. Here are some of the magic components that we glanced over:

- Loading a page before test execution
- Assertion on elements that get loaded in promises

Loading a page before test execution

In the previous test, we used the following code to specify that the browser should point to the home page:

```
browser.get('/');
```

The preceding command will launch the browser and navigate to the `baseUrl` location. Once the browser reaches the page, it will have to load AngularJS and then implement the AngularJS-specific functions. Our tests don't have any wait logic, and this is part of the beauty of Protractor with AngularJS. The waiting for page loading is already built in the framework for you. Your tests can then be written very cleanly.

Assertion on elements that get loaded in promises

The assertions and expectations already have promise fulfillment written in them. In the case of our test, we wrote the assertion so that it expects the count to be three:

```
expect(todoListItems.count()).toBe(3);
```

However, in reality, we may have thought that we needed to add asynchronous testing to the assertion in order to wait for the promise to be fulfilled, something more complicated like the following:

```
it('', function(done){
  var todoListItems = element.all(by.repeater('item in list'));
  todoListItems.count().then(function(count){
    expect(count).toBe(3);
    done();
  });
})
```

The preceding code is longer, more granular, and harder to read. Protractor has the ability for certain elements built in to expectations to make tests more concise.

TDD with Protractor

With our first test, there is a clear distinction of end-to-end tests and unit tests. With the unit test, we focused on strong coupling the test to the code. As an example, our unit test spied on the scope for a specific controller, `TodoController`. We used Angular mocks to initialize the scope with a variable we could then evaluate:

```
inject(function($controller){
  $controller('TodoController',{$scope:scope});
});
```

In the Protractor test, we don't care about which controller we are testing and our focus is on the user perspective of the test. We first start with the selection of a particular element within the **Document Object Model (DOM)**; in our case, that element is tied to AngularJS, `ng-repeat`. The Assert is that the number of elements for a specific repeater is equal to the expected count.

With the loose coupling of the end-to-end test, we can write a test that focuses on the user specification, which initially displays three elements, and then have the freedom to write that in the page, controllers, and so on, in any way we want.

Self-test questions

Use TDD with Protractor to develop the third development to-do list item:

Q1. Protractor uses which of the following frameworks?

1. Selenium
2. Unobtanium
3. Karma

Q2. You can install Angular mocks by running `bower install angular-mocks`.

1. True
2. False

Q3. What steps does the TDD life cycle, discussed in this book, consist of?
1. Test first, make it run, make it better (refactor)
2. Test, make it better (refactor), make it run
3. Make it run, test, make it better

Additionally, if you want more practice, add a functionality to the application to remove an item from the to-do list.

Summary

This chapter has given you the skills necessary to install, configure, and apply TDD principles to end-to-end testing. We have seen how we can leverage the existing TDD life cycle (test, make it run, make it better) and techniques with Protractor. Protractor is an important part of testing any AngularJS application. It bridges the gap to ensure the user's specifications work as expected. When end-to-end tests are written to the user specifications, the confidence of the application and ability to refactor grows. In the upcoming chapters, we will see how to apply Karma and Protractor in more depth with simple straightforward examples. The next chapter will walk you through testing controllers, using Angular mocks, and using Protractor to enter key strokes.

4
The First Step

The first step is always the hardest. This chapter provides an initial introductory walk-through of how to use TDD to build an AngularJS application with a controller, model, and scope. You will be able to begin the TDD journey and see the fundamentals in action. Up to this point, this book has focused on a foundation of TDD and the tools. Now, we will switch gears and dive into TDD with AngularJS. This chapter will be the first step of TDD. We have already seen how to install Karma and Protractor, in addition to small examples and a walk-through on how to apply it. This chapter will focus on the creation of social media comments. It will also focus on the testing associated with controllers and the use of Angular mocks to AngularJS components in a test.

Preparing the application's specification

Create an application to enter comments. The specification of the application is as follows:

- Given I am posting a new comment, when I click on the submit button, the comment should be added to the to-do list
- Given a comment, when I click on the like button, the number of likes for the comment should be increased

Now that we have the specification of application, we can create our development to-do list. It won't be easy to create an entire to-do list of the whole application. Based on the user specifications, we have an idea of what needs to be developed. Here is a rough sketch of the UI:

Hold yourself back from jumping into the implementation and thinking about how you will use a controller with a service, `ng-repeat`, and so on. Resist, resist, resist! Although you can think of how this will be developed in the future, it is never clear until you delve into the code, and that is where you start getting into trouble. TDD and its principles are here to help you get your mind and focus in the right place.

Setting up the project

In previous chapters, we discussed in detail how a project should be set up, explained the different components involved, and walked through the entire process of testing. I will skip these details and provide a list in the following section for the initial actions to get the project set up.

Setting up the directory

The following instructions are specific to setting up the project directory:

1. Create a new project directory.

2. Get `angular` into the project using Bower:

    ```
    bower install angular
    ```

3. Get `angular-mocks` for testing using Bower:

    ```
    bower install angular-mocks
    ```

4. Initialize the application's source directory:

    ```
    mkdir app
    ```

5. Initialize the test directory:

   ```
   mkdir spec
   ```

6. Initialize the unit test directory:

   ```
   mkdir spec/unit
   ```

7. Initialize the end-to-end test directory:

   ```
   mkdir spec/e2e
   ```

Once the initialization is complete, your folder structure should look as follows:

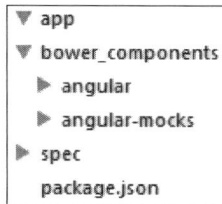

```
▼ app
▼ bower_components
   ▶ angular
   ▶ angular-mocks
▶ spec
   package.json
```

Setting up Protractor

In *Chapter 3, End-to-end Testing with Protractor*, we discussed the full installation and setup of Protractor. In this chapter, we will just discuss the steps at a higher level:

1. Install Protractor in the project:

   ```
   $ npm install protractor
   ```

2. Update Selenium WebDriver:

   ```
   $ ./node_modules/protractor/bin/webdriver-manager update
   ```

   Make sure that Selenium has been installed.

3. Copy the example `chromeOnly` configuration into the root of the project:

   ```
   $ cp ./node_modules/protractor/example/chromeOnlyConf.js .
   ```

4. Configure the Protractor configuration using the following steps:

   1. Open the Protractor configuration.
   2. Edit the Selenium WebDriver location to reflect the relative directory to `chromeDriver`:

      ```
      chromeDriver:
      './node_modules/protractor/selenium/chromedriver',
      ```

3. Edit the `files` section to reflect the test directory:

```
specs: ['spec/e2e/**/*.js'],
```

5. Set the default base URL:

```
baseUrl: 'http://localhost:8080/',
```

Excellent! Protractor should now be installed and set up. Here is the complete configuration:

```
exports.config = {
  chromeOnly: true,
  chromeDriver: './node_modules/protractor/selenium/chromedriver',

  capabilities: {
    'browserName': 'chrome'
  },


  baseUrl: 'http://localhost:8080/',

  specs: ['spec/e2e/**/*.js'],
};
```

Setting up Karma

The details for Karma can be found in *Chapter 2, The Karma Way*. Here is a brief summary of the steps required to install and get your new project set up:

1. Install Karma using the following command:

```
npm install karma -g
```

2. Initialize the Karma configuration:

```
karma init
```

3. Update the Karma configuration:

```
files: [
    'bower_components/angular/angular.js',
    'bower_components/angular-mocks/angular-mocks.js',
    'spec/unit/**/*.js'
],
```

Now that we have set up the project directory and initialized Protractor and Karma, we can dive into the code. Here is the complete `karma.conf.js` file:

```
module.exports = function(config) {
  config.set({

    basePath: '',
    frameworks: ['jasmine'],
    files: [
'bower_components/angular/angular.js',
      'bower_components/angular-mocks/angular-mocks.js',
      'spec/unit/**/*.js'
    ],
    reporters: ['progress'],
    port: 9876,
    autoWatch: true,
    browsers: ['Chrome'],
    singleRun: false
  });
};
```

Setting up http-server

A web server will be used to host the application. As this will just be for local development only, you can use `http-server`. The `http-server` module is a simple HTTP server that serves static content. It is available as an npm module. To install `http-server` in your project, type the following command:

$ npm install http-server

Once `http-server` is installed, you can run the server by providing it with the root directory of the web page. Here is an example:

$ ./node_modules/http-server/bin/http-server

Now that you have `http-server` installed, you can move on to the next step.

Top-down or bottom-up approach

From our development perspective, we have to determine where to start. The approaches that we will discuss in this book are as follows:

- **The bottom-up approach**: With this approach, we think about the different components we will need (controller, service, module, and so on) and then pick the most logical one and start coding.

- **The top-down approach**: With this approach, we work from the user scenario and UI. We then create the application around the components in the application.

There are merits to both types of approaches and the choice can be based on your team, existing components, requirements, and so on. In most cases, it is best for you to make the choice based on the least resistance. In this chapter, the approach of specification is top-down, everything is laid out for us from the user scenario and will allow you to organically build the application around the UI.

Testing a controller

Before getting into the specification, and the mind-set of the feature being delivered, it is important to see the fundamentals of testing a controller. An AngularJS controller is a key component used in most applications.

A simple controller test setup

When testing a controller, tests are centered on the controller's scope. The tests confirm either the objects or methods in the scope. Angular mocks provide `inject`, which finds a particular reference and returns it for you to use. When `inject` is used for the controller, the controllers scope can be assigned to an outer reference for the entire test to use. Here is an example of what this would look like:

```
describe('',function(){
  var scope = {};
  beforeEach(function(){
    module('anyModule');
    inject(function($controller){
      $controller('AnyController',{$scope:scope});
    });
  });
});
```

In the preceding case, the test's `scope` object is assigned to the actual scope of the controller within the inject function. The `scope` object can now be used throughout the test, and is also reinitialized before each test.

Initializing the scope

In the preceding example, `scope` is initialized to an object `{}`. This is not the best approach; just like a page, a controller might be nested within another controller. This will cause inheritance of a parent scope as follows:

```
<body ng-app='anyModule'>
  <div ng-controller='ParentController'>
    <div ng-controller='ChildController'>
    </div>
  </div>
</body>
```

As seen in the preceding code, we have this hierarchy of scopes that the `ChildController` function has access to. In order to test this, we have to initialize the `scope` object properly in the `inject` function. Here is how the preceding scope hierarchy can be recreated:

```
inject(function($controller,$rootScope){
  var parentScope = $rootScope.$new();
$controller('ParentController',{$scope:parentScope});
var childScope = parentScope.$new();
$controller('AnyController',{$scope: childScope});
});
```

There are two main things that the preceding code does:

- The `$rootScope` scope is injected into the test. The `$rootScope` scope is the highest level of scope that exists.
- Each level of scope is created with the `$new()` method. This method creates the child scope.

In this chapter, we will use the simplified version and initialize the scope to an empty object; however, it is important to understand how to create the scope when required.

Bring on the comments

Now that the setup and approach have been decided, we can start our first test. From a testing point of view, as we will be using a top-down approach, we will write our Protractor tests first and then build the application. We will follow the same TDD life cycle we have already reviewed, that is, test first, make it run, and make it better.

Test first

The scenario given is in a well-specified format already and fits our Protractor testing template:

```
describe('',function(){
  beforeEach(function(){
  });
  it('',function(){
  });
});
```

Placing the scenario in the template, we get the following code:

```
describe('Given I am posting a new comment',function(){
  describe('When I push the submit button',function(){
    beforeEach(function(){
    });
    it('Should then add the comment',function(){
    });
  });
});
```

Following the 3 A's (Assemble, Act, Assert), we will fit the user scenario in the template.

Assemble

The browser will need to point to the first page of the application. As the base URL has already been defined, we can add the following to the test:

```
beforeEach(function(){
  browser.get('/');
});
```

Now that the test is prepared, we can move on to the next step, Act.

Act

The next thing we need to do, based on the user specification, is add an actual comment. The easiest thing is to just put some text into an input box. The test for this, again without knowing what the element will be called or what it will do, is to write it based on what it should be.

Here is the code to add the comment section for the application:

```
beforeEach(function(){
    ...
    var commentInput = $('input');
    commentInput.sendKeys('a comment');
});
```

The last assemble component, as part of the test, is to push the **Submit** button. This can be easily achieved in Protractor using the `click` function. Even though we don't have a page yet, or any attributes, we can still name the button that will be created:

```
beforeEach(function(){
    ...
    var submitButton = element.all(by.buttonText('Submit')).click();
});
```

Finally, we will hit the crux of the test and assert the users' expectations.

Assert

The user expectation is that once the **Submit** button is clicked, the comment is added. This is a little ambiguous, but we can determine that somehow the user needs to get notified that the comment was added. The simplest approach is to display all comments on the page. In AngularJS, the easiest way to do this is to add an `ng-repeat` object that displays all comments. To test this, we will add the following:

```
it('Should then add the comment',function(){
    var comments = element(by.repeater('comment in comments')).first();
    expect(comment.getText()).toBe('a comment');
});
```

Now, the test has been constructed and meets the user specifications. It is small and concise. Here is the completed test:

```
describe('Given I am posting a new comment',function(){
    describe('When I push the submit button',function(){
        beforeEach(function(){
        //Assemble
            browser.get('/');

            var commentInput = $('input');
            commentInput.sendKeys('a comment');
```

```
    //Act
    //Act
    var submitButton = element.all(by.buttonText('Submit')).
    click();
  });
  //Assert
  it('Should then add the comment',function(){
  var comments = element(by.repeater('comment in
   comments')).first();
   expect(comment.getText()).toBe('a comment');
  });
 });
});
```

Make it run

Based on the errors and output of the test, we will build our application as we go.

1. The first step to make the code run is to identify the errors. Before starting off the site, let's create a bare bones `index.html` page:

```
<!DOCTYPE html>
<html>
<head>
  <title></title>
</head>
<body>

</body>
</html>
```

Already anticipating the first error, add AngularJS as a dependency in the page:

```
<script type='text/javascript' src='bower_components/angular/
angular.js'></script>
</body>
```

2. Now, starting the web server using the following command:

```
$ ./node_modules/http-server/bin/http-server -p 8080
```

3. Run Protractor to see the first error:

```
$ ./node_modules/.bin/protractor chromeOnlyConf.js
```

4. Our first error states that AngularJS could not be found:

```
Error: Angular could not be found on the page
http://localhost:8080/ : angular never provided
resumeBootstrap
```

This is because we need to add ng-app to the page. Let's create a module and add it to the page.

The complete HTML page now looks as follows:

```
<!DOCTYPE html>
<html>
<head>
  <title></title>
</head>
<body>

    <script src="bower_components/angular/angular.js"></script>
</body>
</html>
```

Adding the module

The first component that you need to define is an ng-app attribute in the index.html page. Use the following steps to add the module:

1. Add ng-app as an attribute to the body tag:

   ```
   <body ng-app='comments'>
   ```

2. Now, we can go ahead and create a simple comments module and add it to a file named comments.js:

   ```
   angular.module('comments',[]);
   ```

3. Add this new file to index.html:

   ```
   <script src='app/commentController.js'></script>
   ```

4. Rerun the Protractor test to get the next error:

   ```
   $ Error: No element found using locator:
   By.cssSelector('input')
   ```

The test couldn't find our input locator. You need to add the input to the page.

Adding the input

Here are the steps you need to follow to add the input to the page:

1. All we have to do is add a simple `input` tag to the page:

   ```
   <input type='text' />
   ```

2. Run the test and see what the new output is:

   ```
   $ Error: No element found using locator:
   by.buttonText('Submit')
   ```

3. Just like the previous error, we need to add a button with the appropriate text:

   ```
   <button type='button'>Submit</button>
   ```

4. Run the test again and the next error is as follows:

   ```
   $ Error: No element found using locator: by.repeater
   ('comment in comments')
   ```

This appears to be from our expectation that a submitted comment will be available on the page through `ng-repeat`. To add this to the page, we will use a controller to provide the data for the repeater.

Controller

As we mentioned in the preceding section, the error is because there is no `comments` object. In order to add the `comments` object, we will use a controller that has an array of comments in its scope. Use the following steps to add a `comments` object in the scope:

1. Create a new file in the app directory named `commentController.js`:

   ```
   angular.module('comments')
   .controller('CommentController', ['$scope',
   function($scope){
        $scope.comments = [];
   }])
   ```

2. Add it to the web page after the AngularJS script:

   ```
   <script src='app/commentController.js'></script>
   ```

3. Now, we can add `commentController` to the page:

   ```
   <div ng-controller='CommentController'>
   ```

4. Then, add a repeater for the comments as follows:

   ```
   <ul ng-repeat='comment in comments'>
     <li>{{comment}}</li>
   </ul>
   ```

5. Run the Protractor test and let's see where we are:

```
$ Error: No element found using locator: by.repeater('comment in comments')
```

Hmmm! We get the same error.

6. Let's look at the actual page that gets rendered and see what's going on. In Chrome, go to `http://localhost:8080` and open the console to see the page source (*Ctrl* + *Shift* + *J*). You should see something like what's shown in the following screenshot:

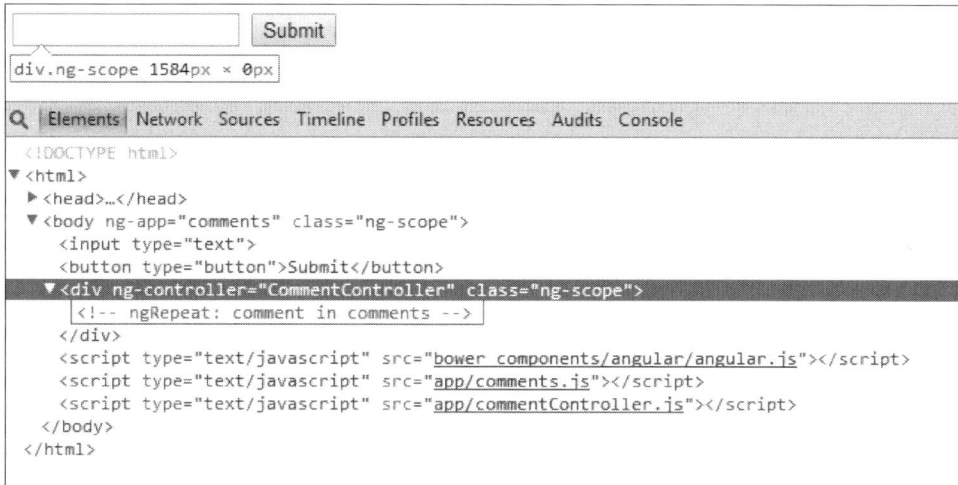

Notice that the repeater and controller are both there; however, the repeater is commented out. Since Protractor is only looking at visible elements, it won't find the repeater.

7. Great! Now we know why the repeater isn't visible, but we have to fix it. In order for a comment to show up, it has to exist on the controller's `comments` scope. The smallest change is to add something to the array to initialize it as shown in the following code snippet:

```
.controller('CommentController',['$scope',function($scope){
  $scope.comments = ['anything'];
}]);
```

8. Now run the test and we get the following:

```
$ Expected 'anything' to be 'a comment'.
```

Wow! We finally tackled all the errors and reached the expectation. Here is what the HTML code looks like so far:

```html
<!DOCTYPE html>
<html>
<head>
  <title></title>
</head>
<body ng-app='comments'>
  <div ng-controller='CommentController'>
    <input type='text' />
    <ul>
      <li ng-repeat='comment in comments'>
        {{comment.value}}
      </li>

    </ul>
  </div>

<script src='bower_components/angular/angular.js'></script>
<script src='app/comments.js'></script>
<script src='app/commentController.js'></script>
</body>
</html>
```

The `comments.js` module looks as follows:

```javascript
angular.module('comments',[]);
```

Here is `commentController.js`:

```javascript
angular.module('comments')
  .controller('CommentController',['$scope', function($scope){
    $scope.comments = [];
  }])
```

Make it pass

With TDD, you want to add the smallest possible component to make the test pass. Since we have hardcoded, for the moment, the comments to be initialized to `anything`, change `anything` to a `comment`; this should make the test pass. Here is the code to make the test pass:

```javascript
angular.module('comments')
.controller('CommentController',['$scope', function($scope){
```

```
    $scope.comments = ['a comment'];
}]);
...
```

Run the test, and bam! We get a passing test:

```
$ 1 test, 1 assertion, 0 failures
```

Wait a second! We still have some work to do. Although we got the test to pass, it is not done. We added some hacks just to get the test passing. The two things that stand out are:

- Clicking on the **Submit** button, which really doesn't have any functionality
- Hardcoded initialization of the expected value for `a comment`

The preceding changes are critical steps we need to perform before we move forward. They will be tackled in the next phase of the TDD life cycle, that is, make it better (refactor).

Make it better

The two components that need to be reworked are:

- Adding behavior to the **Submit** button
- Removing hardcoded value of the comments

Implementing the Submit button

The **Submit** button needs to actually do something. We were able to sidestep the implementation by just hardcoding the value. Using our tried and trusted TDD techniques, switch to an approach focused on unit testing. So far, the focus has been on the UI and pushing changes to the code. We haven't written a single unit test.

For this next bit of work, we will switch gears and focus on driving the development of the **Submit** button through tests. We will be following the TDD life cycle (test first, make it run, make it better).

Configuring Karma

We did something very similar for the to-do list application in *Chapter 2, The Karma Way*. I won't spend as much time diving into the code, so please review the previous chapters for a deeper discussion on some of the attributes. Here are the steps you need to follow to configure Karma:

1. Update the `files` section with the added files:

   ```
   files: [
       ...
       'app/comments.js',
       'app/commentController.js',
       ...
   ],
   ```

2. Start Karma:

   ```
   $ karma start
   ```

3. Confirm that Karma is running:

   ```
   $ Chrome 36.0.1985 (Windows 7): Executed 1 of 1 SUCCESS
   (0.018 secs / 0.015 secs)
   ```

Test first

Let's first start with a new file in the `spec/unit` folder called `comments.js`. We will use the base template:

```
describe('', function(){
  beforeEach(function(){
  });
  it('', function(){
  });
});
```

According to the specification, when the **Submit** button is clicked, it needs to add a comment. We will need to fill in the blanks of the three components of a test (Assemble, Act, Assert).

Assemble

The behavior will need to be part of a controller for the frontend to use it. The object under test in this case is the controller's `scope` object; we will need to add this to the assemble of this test. To wire up the AngularJS controller we need to initialize the module and then inject the `CommentController` scope into the test. As we did in *Chapter 2, The Karma Way*, we will do the same in the following code:

```
var scope = {};
beforeEach(function(){
  module('comments');
  inject(function($controller){
    $controller('CommentController',{$scope:scope});
  });
  ...
})
```

Now, the controller's `scope` object, which is under test, is available to the test.

Act

The specification determines that we need to call a `add` method in the `scope` object. Add the following code to the `beforeEach` section of the test:

```
beforeEach(function(){
  ...
  scope.add('any Comment');
});
```

Now for the assertion.

Assert

Assert that the comment items in the `scope` object now contain `any comment` as the first element. Add the following code to the test:

```
it('',function(){
  expect(scope.comments[0]).toBe('any comment');
});
```

Save the file and let's move on to the next step of the life cycle and make it run (execute).

Make it run

Now that we have most of the test prepared, we need to make the test pass. Looking at the output of the console where Karma is running, we see the following:

```
$ TypeError: undefined is not a function...unit/comments.js:4:9
```

Looking at the line number, that is 4:9, of our unit test, we see that this is the add function. Let's go ahead and put in an add function into the controller's scope object using the following steps:

1. Open the controller scope and create a function named add:

   ```
   $scope.add = function(){}
   ```

2. Check Karma's output and let's see where we are:

   ```
   $ Expected 'a comment' to be 'any comment'.
   ```

3. Now, we have hit the expectation. Remember to think of the smallest change to get this to work. Modify the add function to set the $scope.comments array to any comment when called:

   ```
   $scope.add = function(){
     $scope.comments.unshift('any comment');
   };
   ```

   > Unshift is a standard JavaScript function that adds an item to the front of an array.

4. When we check Karma's output, we see the following:

   ```
   $ Chrome 36.0.1985 (Windows 7): Executed 1 of 1 SUCCESS
   ```

Success! The test passes, but again needs some work. Let's move on to the next stage and make it better (refactor).

Make it better

The main point that needs to be refactored is the add function. It doesn't take any arguments! This should be straightforward to add, and simply confirm that the test still runs. Update the add function of CommentController.js to take an argument and use that argument to add to the comments array:

```
$scope.add = function(commentToAdd){
  $scope.comments.unshift(commentToAdd);
};
```

Check the output window of Karma and ensure that the test still passes. The complete unit test looks as follows:

```
describe('',function(){
  var scope = {};
  beforeEach(function(){
    module('comments');
    inject(function($controller){
      $controller('CommentController', {$scope:scope});
    });

    scope.add('any comment');
  });

  it('',function(){
    expect(scope.comments[0]).toBe('any comment');
  })
});
```

The `CommentController` file now looks as follows:

```
angular.module('comments')
  .controller('CommentController', ['$scope', function($scope){
      $scope.comments = [];
      $scope.add = function(commentToAdd){
          $scope.comments.unshift(newComment);
      };
}]);
```

Back up the test chain

We completed the unit test and addition of the `add` function. Now we can add the function to specify the behavior of the **Submit** button. The way to link the `add` method to the button is to to use the `ng-click` attribute. The steps to add behavior to the **Submit** button are as follows:

1. Open the `index.html` page and link it as follows:

   ```
   <button type="button" ng-click="add('a comment')">
   Submit</button>
   ```

   Warning! Is the value hardcoded? Well, again, we want to do the smallest change and ensure that the test still passes. We will work through our refactors until the code is how we want it, but instead of a big bang approach, we want to make small incremental changes.

2. Now let's rerun the Protractor test and ensure that it still passes. The output says it passes, and we are okay. The hardcoded value wasn't removed from the comments. Let's go ahead and remove that now. The `CommentsController` file should now look as follows:

```
$scope.comments = [];
```

3. Run the test and see that we still get a passing test.

Now the last thing we need to mop up is the hardcoded value in `ng-click`. The comment being added should be determined by the input in the comment input text.

Bind the input

Here are the steps you need to follow to bind the input:

1. To be able to bind the input into something meaningful, add an `ng-model` attribute to the `input` tag:

```
<input type='text' ng-model='newComment'/>
```

2. Then, in the `ng-click` attribute, simply use the `newComment` model as the input:

```
<button type='button' ng-click='add(newComment)'>
Submit</button>
```

Run the Protractor test and confirm that everything has passed and is good to go.

Onwards and upwards

Now that we have the first specification working end-to-end and unit tested, we can start the next specification. The next specification states that the users want the ability to like a comment.

We will use the same top-down approach and start our test from a Protractor test. We will continue to follow the TDD life cycle, that is, test first, make it run, make it better.

Test first

Following the pattern, we will start with a basic Protractor test template:

```
describe('',function(){
  beforeEach(function(){
  });
```

```
  it('', function(){
  });
});
```

When we fill in the specification, we get the following:

```
describe('When I like a comment',function(){
  beforeEach(function(){
  });
  it('should then be liked', function(){
  });
});
```

With the template in place, we are ready to construct the test.

Assemble

The assembly of this test will require a comment to exist. Place the comment within the existing posted comment test. It should look similar to this:

```
describe(''Given I am posting a new comment', function(){
describe('When I like a comment',function(){

  ...

  });
});
```

Act

The user specification we test is that the `like` button performs an action for a specific comment. Here are the steps that will be required and the code required to do them (note that the following steps will be added to the `beforeEach` text):

1. Store the first comment so that it can be used in the test:

   ```
   var firstComment = null;
   beforeEach(function(){

   ...
   ```

2. Find the first comment's like button:

   ```
   var firstComment = element.all(by.repeater('comment in
   comments').first();
   var likeButton = firstComment.element
   (by.buttonText('like'));
   ```

3. The code for the `like` button when it is clicked is as follows:

   ```
   likeButton.click();
   ```

Assert

The specification expectation is that once the comment has been liked, it is liked. This is best done by putting an indicator of the number of likes, and ensuring the count is 1. The code will then be as follows:

```
it('Should increase the number of likes to one',function(){
var commentLikes = firstComment.element(by.binding('likes'));
  expect(commentLikes.getText()).toBe(1);
});
```

The created test now looks as follows:

```
describe('When I like a comment',function(){
  var firstComment = null;
  beforeEach(function(){

    //Assemble
    firstComment = element.all(by.repeater('comment in comments').
    first();
    var likeButton = firstComment.element(by.buttonText('like'));

    //Act
    likeButton.click();
  });

  //Assert
  it('Should increase the number of likes to one', function(){
    var commentLikes = firstComment.element(by.binding('likes'));
    expect(commentLikes.getText()).toBe(1);
});;});
```

Make it run

The test has been prepared and is itching to run. We will now run the test and fix the code until the test passes. The following steps will detail the error and the fix cycle required to make the test path:

1. Run Protractor.
2. View the error message in the command line:

```
$ Error: No element found using locator: by.buttonText("like")
```

3. As the error states, there is no `like` button. Go ahead and add the button:

```
<li ng-repeat='comment in comments'>
{{comment}}
  <button type="button">like</button>
</li>
```

4. Run Protractor.

5. View the next error message:

```
$ Expected 'a comment like' to be 'a comment'.
```

6. By adding the `like` button, we caused our other test to fail. The reason is our use of the `getText()` method. Protractor's `getText()` method gets the inner text including inner elements. To fix this, we will need to update the previous test to include `like` as part of the test:

```
it('Should then add the comment',function(){
var comments = element.all(by.repeater('comment in comments')).
first();
expect(comments.getText()).toBe('a comment like');
});
```

7. Run Protractor.

8. View the next error message:

```
$ Error: No element found using locator: by.binding("likes")
```

9. Time to add a `likes` binding. This one is a little more involved. Likes needs to be bound to a comment. We need to change the way the comments are held in the controller. Comments need to hold the `comment` value and the number of likes. A comment should be an object like this: `{value:'',likes:0}`. Again, the focus of this step is just to get the test to pass. The next step is to update the controller's `add` function to create comments based on the object we described in the preceding steps. Open `commentController.js` and edit the `add` function as follows:

```
$scope.add = function(commentToAdd){
var newComment = {value:commentToAdd,likes:0};
  $scope.comments.unshift(newComment);
};
```

10. Update the page to use the value for the comment:

```
<li ng-repeat='comment in comments'>
{{comment.value}}
```

11. Before rerunning the Protractor test, we need to add the new `comment.likes` binding to the HTML page:

```
<li ng-repeat='comment in comments'>
...
{{comment.likes}}
```

12. Now rerun the Protractor tests and let's see where the errors are:

```
$ Expected 'a comment like 0' to be 'a comment like'
```

13. Because the inner text of the comment has changed, we need to change the expectation of the test:

```
it('Should then add the comment', function(){
...
    expect(comments.getText()).toBe('a comment like 0');
});
```

14. Run Protractor:

```
$ Expected '0' to be '1'.
```

15. Now, we are finally down to the expectation of the test. In order to make this test pass, the smallest change will be to make the `like` button update the likes on the `comment` array. The first step is to add a `like` method on the controller, which will update the number of likes:

```
$scope.like = function(comment){
comment.likes++;
};
```

16. Link the `like` method to the HTML page using an `ng-click` attribute on the button as follows:

```
<button type="button" ng-click='like(comment)'>
like</button>
```

17. Run Protractor and confirm that the tests pass!

The page now looks as follows:

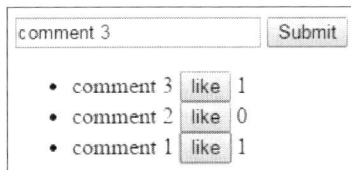

Compared to the drawing at the beginning of this chapter, all the features have been created. Now that we made the test pass in Protractor, we need to check the unit tests to ensure that our changes didn't break the unit tests.

Fixing the unit tests

One of the primary changes required was to make the comment an object, consisting of a value and number of likes. Before thinking too much about how the unit tests could have been affected, let's kick them off. Execute the following command:

```
$ karma start
```

As expected, the error is related to the new comment object:

```
$ Expected { value : 'any comment', likes : 0 } to be 'any comment'.
```

Reviewing the expectation, it seems like the only thing required is for comment. value to be used in the expectation as opposed to the comment object itself. Change the expectation as follows:

```
it('',function(){
var firstComment = scope.comments[0];
expect(firstComment.value).toBe('any comment');
})
```

Save the file and check the Karma output. Confirm that the test passes. Both the Karma and Protractor tests pass and we have completed the primary user behaviors of adding a comment and liking it. You are free now to move on to the next step and make things better.

Make it better

All in all, the approach ended up with the result we wanted. Users are now able to like a comment in the UI and see the number of likes. The major callout from a refactor standpoint is that we have not unit tested the like method. Reviewing our development to-do list, we see that the to-do list is an action we wrote down. Before completely wrapping up the feature, let's discuss the option of adding a unit test for the like functionality.

Coupling of the test

As already discussed in this book, tests are tightly coupled to the implementation. This is a good thing when there is a complicated logic involved or you need to ensure that certain aspects of the application behave in certain ways. It is important to be aware of the coupling and know when it is important to bring it into the application and when it is not. The `like` function we created simply increments a counter on an object. This can be easily tested; however, the coupling we will bring in with a unit test will not give us the extra value. In this case, we will not add an additional unit test for the `like` method. As the application progresses, we may find the need to add a unit test in order to develop and extend the function. Here are a couple of things I consider when adding a test:

- Does adding a test outweigh the cost of maintaining a test?
- Is the test adding value to the code?
  - Does it help other developers better understand the code?
- Is the functionality being tested in some other way?

Based on our decision, there is no more refactoring or testing required. In the next section, we will take a step back and review the main points of this chapter.

Self-test questions

Q1. The `$new` function is used to create a child scope: `$scope.$new`.

1. True
2. False

Q2. Given the following code segment, how would you select the items in the list?

```
<ul>
<li ng-repeat="item in myItems">
{{item.value}}
</li
</ul>
```

1. `element.all(by.repeater('item in items')).`
2. `element.all(by.repeater('item in myItems')).`
3. `element.all('item in items').`

Q3. The Angular mocks `inject` function is used to:

1. Resolve application dependencies/references.

2. Inject dependencies into the application.

3. None of the above.

Summary

In this chapter, we walked through the TDD techniques of using Protractor and Karma together. As the application was developed, you were able to see where, why, and how to apply the TDD testing tools and techniques. The approach, top-down, was different than the bottom-up approach discussed in *Chapter 2, The Karma Way* and *Chapter 3, End-to-end Testing with Protractor*. With the bottom-up approach, the specifications are used to build unit tests and then build the UI layer on top of that. In this chapter, a top-down approach was shown to focus on the user's behavior. The top-down approach tests the UI and then filters the development through the other layers. Both approaches have their merit. When applying TDD, it is essential to know how to use both. In addition to walking through a different TDD approach, you saw some of the core testing components of AngularJS such as:

*   Testing a controller from end-to-end and unit perspectives
*   Using Angular mocks to test the `scope` object of a controller
*   Protractor's ability to:
    *   Bind to `ng-repeater` and `ng-model`
    *   Send key strokes to input columns
    *   Get an element's text by its inner HTML code and all subelements

The next chapter will build on the techniques used here and look into headless browser testing, advanced techniques for Protractor, and how to test AngularJS routes.

5
Flip Flop

At this point, you should be feeling confident in the initial implementation of an AngularJS application using TDD. You should be familiar with using a test-first approach. In this chapter, you will continue to expand your knowledge of applying TDD with AngularJS by looking at the following:

- AngularJS routes
- Partial views
- Protractor location references with **CSS (Cascading Style Sheets)** and HTML elements
- Headless browser testing with Karma

Fundamentals

This chapter will walk you through applying TDD to routes and partial views for a search application. Before getting into the walk-through, you need to be aware of some of the techniques, configurations, and functions that will be used throughout this chapter, which include:

- Protractor locators
- Headless browser testing

After you have reviewed these concepts, you can move on to the walk-through.

Protractor locators

Protractor locators are key components that you must take time to learn. This book will not be able to show examples of all the different locators, but it will provide examples of the most common ones.

Protractor locators allow you to find elements within an HTML page. In this chapter, you will see the following in action: CSS, HTML, and AngularJS-specific locators. Locators are passed to the `element` function. The `element` function will find and return elements in a page. The generic locator syntax is as follows:

```
element(by.<LOCATOR>);
```

In the preceding code, `<LOCATOR>` is a placeholder. The following sections describe a couple of these locators.

CSS locators

CSS is used to add layout, color, formatting, and style to an HTML page. From an end-to-end testing perspective, the look and style of an element may be part of a specification. As an example consider the following HTML snippet:

```
<div class="anyClass" id="anyId"></div>
// ...
var e1 = element(by.css('.anyClass'));
var e2 = element(by.css('#anyId'));
var e3 = element(by.css('div'));
var e4 = $('div');
```

All four selections will select the div element.

Button and link locators

Besides being able to select and interpret the way something looks, it is also important to be able to find buttons and links within a page. This will allow a test to interact with the site easily. Here are a couple of examples:

- Button text locator:

```
<button>anyButton</button>
// ...
var b1 = element(by.buttonText('anyButton'));
```

- Link text locator:

```
<a href="#">anyLink</a>
// ...
var a1 = element(by.linkText('anyLink'));
```

Angular locators

One of Protractor's key strengths is that it provides testing functionality specific to AngularJS. The repeater locator will select the elements within the application where ng-repeat was used. This is especially useful when looking at the number of returned results and the values of individual results. One key to using this locator is that the string of the repeater locator must match the ng-repeat string used in the AngularJS application. Here is an example of using the repeater locator:

```
//The List in the application to use ng-repeat on
<li ng-repeat="item in list">
  <div>
    <a href="#">link</a>
  </div>
</li>
// ...
var firstItem = element.all(by.repeater
('item in list')).first();
```

The preceding code highlights how to find the first element in a repeater. It should be clear that in this case, the element.all function finds all the elements matching the selector. Then, the first() method is used to return the first element found.

URL location references

When testing AngularJS routes, you need to be able to test the URL of your test. By adding tests around the URL and location, you ensure that the application follows specific routes. This is important because routes provide an interface into your application. Here is how to get the URL reference in a Protractor test:

```
var location = browser.getLocationAbsUrl();
```

Now that you have seen how to use the different locators it is time to put the knowledge to use.

Creating a new project

It is important to get a process and method to set up your projects quickly. The less time you're thinking of the structure of the directory and the required tools, the more time you're developing!

Some people use the angular-seed (`https://github.com/angular/angular-seed`) project, Yeoman, or create a custom template. Although these techniques are useful and have their merit, when starting out in AngularJS, it is essential to understand what it takes to build an application from the ground up. By building the directory structure and installing tools yourself, you will understand AngularJS better. You will be able to make layout decisions based on your specific application and needs, as opposed to fitting into some other mold. As you grow and become a better AngularJS developer, this step may not be needed and will become second nature to you.

In previous chapters, we discussed how to get the project set up, explained the different components involved, and walked through the entire process. I will skip these details and expect that you can recall how to perform the necessary installation. To confirm the installation, here is a screenshot of the expected output:

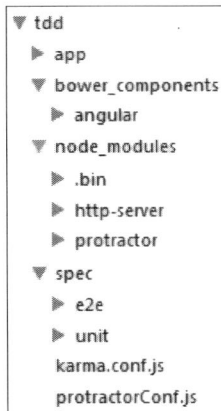

```
▼ tdd
  ▶ app
  ▼ bower_components
    ▶ angular
  ▼ node_modules
    ▶ .bin
    ▶ http-server
    ▶ protractor
  ▼ spec
    ▶ e2e
    ▶ unit
  karma.conf.js
  protractorConf.js
```

Setting up headless browser testing for Karma

In previous chapters, you were running Karma using the default configuration. The default Chrome configuration launches Chrome on every test. Testing against the actual code and browser, which the application will run in, is a powerful tool. However, when launching, a browser may not be how you always wanted it. From a unit test perspective, you may not want the browser to be launched in a window. Some of the reasons are tests may take a long time to run or you may not always have a browser installed.

Luckily, Karma comes equipped with the ability to easily configure PhantomJS, a headless browser. A headless browser runs in the background and will not display web pages in a UI. The PhantomJS headless browser is a really great tool to use for testing. It can even be set up to take screenshots of your tests! Read more about how this is done and the WebKit used on the PhantomJS site at `http://phantomjs.org/`. The succeeding setup configuration will show you how to set up PhantomJS with Karma to get headless browser testing.

Preconfiguration

When Karma is installed, it automatically includes the PhantomJS browser plugin. For your reference, the plugin is located at `https://github.com/karma-runner/karma-phantomjs-launcher`. There shouldn't be any additional installation or configuration required. However, if your setup states that it is missing `karma-phantomjs-launcher`, you can easily install it using `npm`:

```
$ npm install karma-phantomjs-launcher
```

Configuration

PhantomJS is configured in the `browser` section of the Karma configuration. Open the `karma.conf` file and update it with the following details:

```
browsers: ['PhantomJS'],
```

Now that the project has been initialized and configured with headless browser testing, you can see it in action through the following walk-throughs.

Walk-through of Angular routes

This walk-through will leverage AngularJS routes. Routes are an extremely useful feature of AngularJS. They allow you to control certain aspects of the application using different views. This walk-through will flip between views to show you how to use TDD to build routes. The following are the specifications:

- Given a view A that has a single button; the following actions will take place:
    - The button is pushed
    - The view is switched to view B

- Given a view B that has a single button; the following actions will take place:
  - The button is pushed
  - The view is switched to view A

Essentially, this will be an application that does a flip flop between views.

Setting up AngularJS routes

Before you use AngularJS routes, you need to install the AngularJS route component. You can install AngularJS routes using bower as follows:

```
$ bower install angular-route
```

Angular routes requires Angular, as you can imagine. In order to use it an HTML page would look as follows:

```
<!DOCTYPE html>
<html>
<head>
  <title></title>
</head>
<body>
<script src="bower_components/angular/angular.js">
</script>
<script
src="bower_components/angular-route/angular-route.js"></script>

</body>
</html>
```

Defining directions

A route specifies a specific location and expects a result. From an AngularJS perspective, the routes must first be specified and then associated to certain elements within them.

Configuring ngRoute

In order to use AngularJS routes, we first need to bring ngRoute in as a dependency into the application. In app/flipFlop.js, modify the code to bring in ngRoute as a dependency and return the module:

```
var flipFlop = angular.module('flipFlop',['ngRoute']);
```

Now, the second thing required is we need to configure the routes that we need. In our case, we need two routes: one for `viewA` and one for `viewB`. The route configuration will then look as follows:

```
flipFlop.config(['$routeProvider',function($routeProvider){
  $routeProvider
  .when('/view/a',{
    templateUrl : 'app/viewA.html',
    controller : 'ViewAController'
  })
  .when('/view/b',{
    templateUrl : 'app/viewB.html',
    controller : 'ViewBController'
  })
  .otherwise({
    redirectTo : '/view/a'
  });
}]);
```

A route is defined using `when`, which has a first argument as a string for the full route. The second argument is an object, which takes the HTML page for the route (template URL) and the controller for the route (controller).

Defining the route controllers

For both routes, create an empty controller so that it can be a placeholder for the future controller. Here are the steps you need to follow to define route controllers:

1. Create a new file for the View A controller (`/app/ViewAController.js`):

    ```
    angular.module('flipFlop')
      .controller('ViewAController', ['$scope',function($scope){
        }]);
    ```

2. Create another new file for the View B controller (`/app/ViewBController.js`):

    ```
    angular.module('flipFlop')
      .controller('ViewBController', ['$scope',function($scope){
        }]);
    ```

3. Add the two controllers to the `index.html` page:

    ```
    <script src="app/viewAController.js"></script>
    <script src="app/viewBController.js"></script>
    ```

Defining the route views

Route views are partial HTML elements that can be dynamically placed into an application. For the two views we require, we will put a basic `div` tag for each view, as shown in the following steps:

1. Create a new file for `app/viewA.html`:

   ```
   <div id="viewA"></div>
   ```

2. Create a new file for `app/viewB.html`:

   ```
   <div id="viewB"></div>
   ```

The last thing required is to put a placeholder where the route view will be placed in the `index.html` page:

```
<div ng-view></div>
```

Now, the routes are set up with the initial views and controllers. We can continue with the Protractor test.

Assembling the flip flop test

Following the first of the 3 A's, Assemble, the following steps will show you how to assemble the test.

1. Start with the Protractor base template:

   ```
   describe('Given a view A that has a single button',
   function(){
     describe('When the button is pushed',function(){
       beforeEach(function(){
       })
       it(''should be switched to view B'', function(){
       })
     })
   })
   ```

2. Navigate to the root of the application using the following code:

   ```
   browser.get('/index.html');
   ```

3. The `beforeEach` method needs to confirm that the correct view is being displayed. This can be done using a CSS locator to look for the `div` tag of `viewA`. The expectation will look as follows:

   ```
   var viewA = element(by.css('#viewA'));
   expect(viewA.isPresent()).toBeTruthy();
   ```

4. Then, add an expectation that viewB is not visible:

```
var viewB = element(by.css('#viewB'));
expect(viewB.isPresent()).toBeFalsy();
```

You will notice how the selection of viewA and viewB is done outside of the beforeEach method, so it can be used for other expectations.

Making the views flip

The preceding test needs to confirm that when the flip button is pushed, the view should switch. In order to test this, you can use the by.buttonText locator. Here is what it will look like:

```
var buttonToPush = element(by.linkText('flip'));
buttonToPush.click();
```

The beforeEach function is now complete and looks as follows:

```
var viewA = element(by.css('#viewA'));
var viewB = element(by.css('#viewB'));
beforeEach(function(){
  browser.get('/index.htm');
  expect(viewA.isPresent()).toBeTruthy();
  var buttonToPush = element(by.linkText('flip'));
  buttonToPush.click();
})
```

Now, you can add the assertion.

Asserting a flip

The assertion will again use Protractor's CSS locator to find that viewB is available:

```
it('should be switched to view B',function(){
  expect(viewB.isPresent()).toBeTruthy();
})
```

You also need to confirm that viewA is no longer available. Add the expectation that viewA should not exist:

```
it('should not display view A',function(){
  expect(viewA.isPresent()).toBeFalsy();
})
```

The test has now been assembled.

Making flip flop run

Now, you will see the steps required to make the flip flop run:

1. In a new console window, start `http-server`:

   ```
   $ ./node_modules/http-server/bin/http-server -p 8080
   ```

2. Run Protractor:

   ```
   $ ./node_modules/protractor/bin/protractor protractorConf.js
   ```

3. The first error states `Error: Angular could not be found on the page http://localhost:8080/ : angular never provided resumeBootstrap.` When you get this error, proceed with the following steps:

   1. This error means that no AngularJS application has been associated with the application. It's now time to create the application module and add it to the page.

   2. Create a new file named `/app/flipFlop.js`:

      ```
      angular.module('flipFlop',[]);
      ```

   3. Add the new module to the `index.html` page:

      ```
      <script src="app/flipFlop.js"></script>
      ```

   4. Add the AngularJS application identifier to the page:

      ```
      <body ng-app='flipFlop'>
      ```

   5. Rerun the Protractor test.

4. The error is `Error: No element found using locator: by.linkText("flip")`. To rectify this perform the following steps:

   1. Open up the `app/viewA.html` file and add a link to the View B route with the flip text:

      ```
      <div id="viewA">
        <a href="#/view/b">flip</button>
      </div>
      ```

   2. Rerun the test.

5. The Protractor tests now pass.

Making flip flop better

For practice, you should add a link to switch back to `viewA` from `viewB`. There is nothing that has been called out that needs to be changed or refactored. The main takeaway from this walk-through is how to use Protractor to test routes. Here are some screenshots of the application:

- The initial index page is shown in the following screenshot:

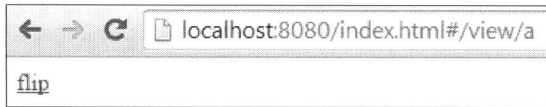

- The following is what you'll see after the view has been switched:

Searching the TDD way

This walk-through will show you how to build a simple search application. The walk-through has two components. The first discusses a search query component. The second uses routes to display search result details.

Deciding on the approach

This walk-through uses the top-down TDD approach. It starts with writing failing tests, from the UI point of view using Protractor, and then working through the application with a combination of unit and end-to-end tests.

Walk-through of search query

The application being built is a search application. The first step is to set up the search area with search results. Imagine I am performing a search. The following actions will occur:

- A search query is typed in
- Results are displayed on the left sidebar

This piece of the application is very similar to the test, layout, and approach you saw in *Chapter 4*, *First Steps*. The application will need to use an input, respond to a click, and confirm the resulting data. Since the tests and code use the same functionality as the previous example, it is not worth providing a complete walk-through of the search functionality. Instead, the following section will show the resulting code with a few explanations.

The search query test

The following code represents the test for the search query functionality:

```
describe('', function(){
    //Store the searchResult for use in the test
    var searchResult = null;
    beforeEach(function(){

    //ASSEMBLE
    browser.get('/index.html');
    var searchResult = element.all(by.repeater('result in results'));
    expect(searchResult.count()).toBe(0);

    //ACT
    var searchQueryInput = $('input');
    searchQueryInput.sendKeys('any value');
    var searchButton = element(by.buttonText('search'));
        searchButton.click();
    });

    //Assert
    it('', function(){
        expect(searchResult.count()).toBe(1);
    });
});
```

You should notice a parallel to previous tests. The functionality is written to mirror the behavior of a user typing in the search box. The test finds the input field, types a value, and then selects the button that says **Search**. The assertion confirms that the result contains a single value. The next section will look at the application from the HTML page.

The search query HTML page

The following code shows the resulting body of the search query HTML page:

```
<body ng-app="search">
  <div ng-controller="SearchController">
    <input type="text" ng-model="searchQuery"></input>
    <button ng-click="search(searchQuery)">search</button>
    <ul>
      <li ng-repeat="result in results">{{result}}</li>
    </ul>
  </div>

  <script src="bower_components/angular/angular.js"></script>
  <script src="app/search.js"></script>
  <script src="app/searchController.js"></script>
</body>
```

The main highlights of the HTML page are:

- The use of the `searchController` class' model to store the `searchQuery` class in the input:

  ```
  <input type="text" ng-model="searchQuery"></input>
  ```

- Associating the button click event to the `searchController`'s search function:

  ```
  <button ng-click="search(searchQuery)">search</button>
  ```

The next section will show the resulting search module and `searchController`.

The search application

Here is the result of the `searchModule` code:

```
var searchModule = angular.module('search',[]);
```

Here is the result of the `searchController` code:

```
angular.module('search')
  .controller('SearchController',['$scope', function($scope){
      $scope.results = [];
      $scope.search = function(){
          $scope.results = ['Any Value'];
      };
  }]);
```

The preceding AngularJS components are similar to what has already been shown in previous chapters. Now that you have reviewed the existing search piece of the application, you can walk through the steps to display search result detail views. Here is what the search application looks like so far:

Show me some results!

Now that the **Search** button is set with the required features, the resulting details need to be displayed when a search result is selected. Here is the user specification. Given the following search results:

- I select an item from the search results

- I will see the details in the main page component

Following the top-down approach, the first step will be the Protractor tests followed by the necessary steps to get the application fully functional.

Creating the search result routes

This application will use routes to switch between views. As this step is primarily about configuration, it doesn't make sense to wait until a test fails. The following steps will briefly recap the necessary steps, as you have already walked through the steps with the flip flop application:

1. Install `angular-routes` using Bower:

   ```
   $ bower install angular-route
   ```

2. Add `angular` and `angular-route` to the `index.html` page:

   ```
   <script src="bower_components/angular
   /angular.js"></script>
   <script src="bower_components/angular-route/angular-
   route.js"></script>
   ```

3. Create a `ngRoute` module as a dependency in the application (`app/search.js`):

   ```
   var searchModule = angular.module('search',['ngRoute']);
   ```

4. Configure the routes in the `app/search.js` file. Add the following route configuration:

```
searchModule.config(['$routeProvider',function($routeProvider){
  $routeProvider
  .when('/splash',{
    templateUrl : 'app/splash.html',
    controller : 'SplashController'
  })
  .when('/detail/:id',{
    templateUrl : 'app/searchDetail.html',
    controller : 'SearchDetailController'
  })
  .otherwise({
    redirectTo : '/splash'
  });
}]);
```

The preceding configuration contains two routes. One for a splash screen/landing page that will be displayed when the user first comes to the page. The second is the route to get the search details.

5. Add the route stub controllers:

   1. Create a new file for SplashController (`app/splashController.js`):

   ```
   angular.module('search')
     .controller('SplashController',['$scope',function($scope){
     }]);
   ```

   2. Create a new file for `SearchDetailController` (`app/searchDetailController.js`):

   ```
   angular.module('search')
     .controller('SearchDetailController',['$scope',function($scope){
     }]);
   ```

6. Add the detail controller to the `index.html` page:

   ```
   <script src="app/searchDetailController.js"></script>
   ```

7. Create the partial view HTML files by following these steps:

   1. Create a new file for `splash.html`:

   ```
   <div id="splash"></div>
   ```

   2. Create a new file for `searchDetail.html`:

   ```
   <div id="searchResultDetail"></div>
   ```

The routes for the test have now been created. You can continue to the next step and begin adding the functionality to link search results to the result details.

Testing the search results

As the specification states, you will need to leverage the existing search results. Instead of creating a test from scratch, you can add to the existing search query test. Start with a base test embedded in the search query test as follows:

```
describe('Given I am searching',function(){
  describe(''when I type in a search query'',function(){
    ...
    describe('Given search results',function(){
      describe('When I select an item from the search
      results',function(){
        beforeEach(function(){
        });
        it('should see the details in the main page
        component',function(){
        });
      });
    });
  })
})
```

Now move on to the next step and build the test.

Assembling the search result test

In this case, the search results are already available from the search query test. You don't have to add any more setup step for the test.

Selecting a search result

The object under test is the result. The test is when the result is selected and then the application must do something. The steps to write this in Protractor are as follows:

1. Find a result item using the following code:

```
var resultItem = element(by.repeater('result in
results')).first();
```

2. Select the result item. As you will be representing the details using a route, you will create a link to the details page and click on the link. Here are the steps to create a link:

    1. Select the link within the result item. This uses the element currently selected and then finds any subelements that meet the criteria. The code for this is as follows:

        ```
        var resultLink = resultItem.element(by.css('a'));
        ```

    2. Now to select the link add the following code:

        ```
        resultLink.click();
        ```

Confirming a search result

Now that the search item has been selected, you will need to verify that the result details page is visible. The simplest solution at this point is to ensure that the details view is visible. This can be done using Protractor's CSS locator to look for the search detail view. The following is the code to be added for confirming a search result:

```
it('Should see the details in the main page component',function(){
    var resultDetail = element(by.css('#searchResultDetail'))
    expect(resultDetail.isDisplayed()).toBeTruthy();
})
```

Here is the complete test:

```
...
describe('When I select an item from the search results', function(){
    beforeEach(function(){
    var resultItem = element.all(by.repeater('result in results')).
first();
    var resultLink = resultItem.element(by.css('a'));
    resultLink.click();
    });
    it('Should see the details in the main page component',function(){
        var resultDetail = element(by.css('#searchResultDetail'))
        expect(resultDetail.isDisplayed()).toBeTruthy();
    });
});
```

Now that the test is set up, you can continue to the next phase of the life cycle and make it run.

Making the search result test run

For this step of the life cycle, we will execute Protractor and make fixes in the application in order to make the test run successfully. Here are the steps you need to follow:

1. The first error : `Error: No element found using locator:`
    `by.cssSelector('a')`

    ◦   We need to add a link to the result item list, which will point to the details of the result. In terms of Angular routes, we will add `#/detail/:resultId` as a prefix:

    ```
    <li ng-repeat="result in results"><a href="#/detail/
    {{result.id}}">{{result.name}}</a></li>
    ```

2. Now rerun the test and we get `UnknownError: unknown error: Element is not clickable at point (48, 57). Other element would receive the click:....`

    ◦   This error is not as clear. When this happens, and the error is not as specific as required, you can jump to the site itself and look at the JavaScript console for errors. Go to `http://localhost:8080`. Here is a screenshot of what you should see:

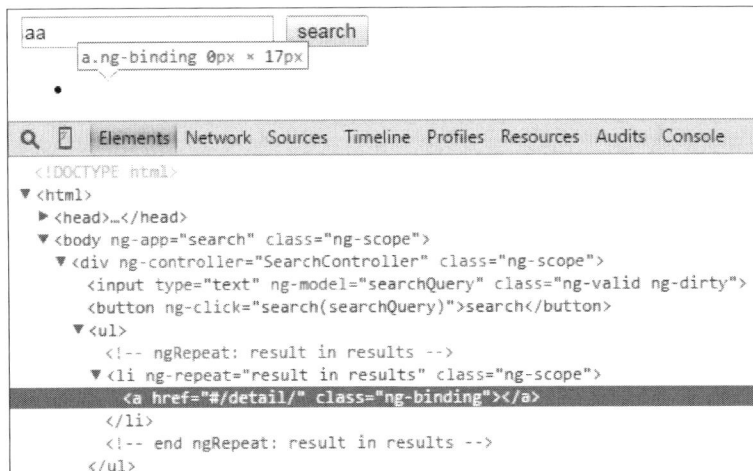

    ◦   The main problem is that the link is not on the page. Looking back at the code, you can see that the search result object is an array of strings but it needs to be an array of objects that have an ID and name.

       °   Update the `app/searchController.js` search function as follows:

```
$scope.search = function(){
    $scope.results = [{id:1,name:'Any Value'}];
};
```

       °   Now rerun the test.

3. The routes have now been configured to the new route (`#/detail/`
   `{{result.id}}`) and the tests now pass.

Creating a location-aware test

As the application uses routes, the route detail view will need to be tested. In this case, you will need to ensure the URL has the ID of the search result. Follow these steps to add the test:

1. In the `beforeEach` method, retrieve the ID of the search result based on `href` of the link attribute:

```
var resultId = null;
beforeEach(function(){
...
resultId = resultLink.getAttribute('href').then(function(attr) {
return attr.match(/#\/detail\/(\d+)/)[1];
});
});
```

2. Resolve the `resultId` promise containing the ID of the result:

```
it('Should set the url to the selected detail view',function(){
resultId.then(function(id) {
```

3. Within the promise, create `expectedUrl`:

```
var expectedUrl = '/detail/'+id;
```

4. Get the location of the URL:

```
browser.getLocationAbsUrl()
```

5. Use the promise to check the expectation on the URL:

```
.then(function(url) {
expect(url.split('#')[1]).toBe(expectedUrl);
});
});
```

Location-aware tests can be very helpful when dealing with routes. The tests can be simple or complex, but help align the route interface to clear specifications.

Making the search result better

Now that there is a passing test, some cleanup and refactoring is needed. There are two primary callouts:

- No unit tests.

- How do you know `searchResultDetail` is specific to the search result we select?

Up to this point, there hasn't been a need to create unit tests to build the application. The focus has been on the UI in the application. There hasn't been logic or actions needed to build on the backend. Most of the development has been focused on wiring up the frontend and making sure the components in the specification are available to the user.

The other action that you need to look at is the fact that there is not a way to test that a loaded view actually reflects data from the selected result. This can be tackled in two parts. The first part is to ensure that the URL for the window points to the correct route. The second part will be to display the ID number of the search result on the view.

Confirming the route ID

The ID will not be displayed to the users; however, it is still an integral part of the application. As the application grows in the following chapters, you will be leveraging the ID to extract further data. This walk-through will follow the TDD life cycle and use Karma to build the feature.

Setting up the route ID unit test

To inject the scope into a controller, the initial test will look as follows:

```
describe('',function(){
  var scope = {};
  beforeEach(function(){
    module('search');
    inject(function($controller){
      $controller('SearchController',{$scope:scope});
    });
  });
  it('',function(){});
});
```

In order to test the routes, the test will leverage the $routeParams object. The $routeParams object gives an object access to information relating to the route that brought the application to the location. For example, the /detail/:id route definition and the /detail/123, $routeParams route will give you the {id:123} object. For the test, a fake $routeParams object containing the ID of the detail object will be used. Update the test so that it has the following fake $routeParams object, which will return an ID of 1:

```
beforeEach(function(){
// ...
var routeParams = {id:1};
$controller('SearchDetailController',{$scope:scope,
$routeParams: routeParams });
```

Now that the fake $routeParams object has been injected into the controller, you can continue to the next phase and make the assertion.

Confirming the ID

The assertion is that the scope has a detail object with the same ID that $routeParams specified. The code for confirming the ID is as follow:

```
it('Should return results',function(){
expect(scope.detail.id).toBe(1);
});
```

Making the route parameter's test run

Now that Karma is running using a headless browser, we can start Karma in the console and let it run as we walk through the issues, as shown in the following steps:

1. Start Karma:

    $ karma start

2. The first issue we get is that ngRoute can't be found. This is because we added angular-route to the project, but haven't added it to karma.conf. Update the karma.conf update the files section with the following code:

    ```
    files: [
    // ...
    'bower_components/angular-route/angular-route.js',
    ```

3. After rerunning the test, we are left with `TypeError: ''undefined'' is not an object (evaluating scope.detail.id)`. To rectify this, perform the following steps:

   1. This error informs us that the `scope.detail.id` object doesn't exist in the controller. We will now update the controller to include it. The first step to fixing this is to add `$routeParams` to `searchDetailController`:

      ```
      .controller('SearchDetailController',['$scope','$routeParams
      ',function($scope,$routeParams){
      ```

   2. Now, in the controller, create the detail object with the `$routeParams` ID:

      ```
      $scope.detail = {id : $routeParams.id};
      ```

   3. The detail object has now been created using the ID of the route. Go ahead and rerun the test.

The test passes!

The application now looks like what is shown in the following screenshot when you first open it:

After a search query, the application looks like what is shown in the following screenshot:

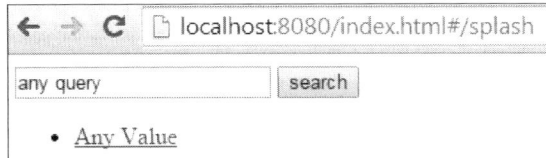

For details of the application looks as shown in the following screenshot (notice that the URL contains the detail route):

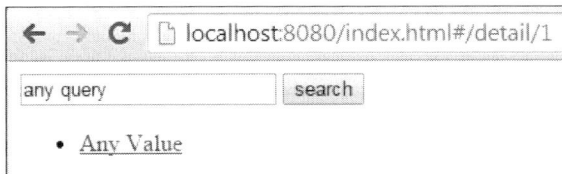

Self-test questions

Q1. Given the following HTML code, how would you select the second list item?

```
<ul>
<li>item 1</li>
<li>item 2</li>
</ul>
```

1. `element.all(by.css('li')).second();`.

2. `element (by.repeater('item in list'))[1];`.

3. `element.all(by.css('li')).get(1);`.

Q2. Given the following AngularJS component, how would you select the element and simulate a click?

```
<a href="#">Some Link</a>
```

1. `$('a').click();`.

2. `element(by.css('li')).click();`.

3. `element(by.linkText('Some Link')).click();`.

Q3. When using routes with AngularJS you need to install `angular-route`.

1. True.

2. False.

Summary

This chapter has shown you how to use TDD to build an AngularJS application. The approach, up to this point, has focused on the specification from a user perspective and using TDD from top-down approach. This technique helps you get usable, small components tested and completed for the users. As applications grow, so does their complexity. As we move on to the next chapter, we will explore the bottom-up approach and see when to use that technique over a top-down approach.

This chapter has shown you how TDD can be used to develop route-based views. This includes utilizing multiple controllers and views. Routes allow you to get a nice separation of your components and views. We have shown the usage of several Protractor locators, from CSS, to repeaters, to link text, to inner locators. Besides using Protractor, we have also learned how to configure Karma with a headless browser, and we got to see it in action.

6
Telling the World

The buildup of TDD focused on fundamental components, namely life cycle and process, using step-by-step walk-throughs. You have taken several applications from the ground up, understanding how to build AngularJS applications and use tools to test them. It is time to expand further into the depths of AngularJS and integrate services, broadcasting, and routes.

This chapter will be slightly different than the others in two ways:

- Instead of building a brand new application, we will use the search application from *Chapter 5*, *Flip Flop*.
- Also, a bottom-up approach will be used. This consists of creating unit tests first and then moving to the UI.

Before the plunge

Before the walk-through, the core concepts of the chapter will be reviewed first. It is important that you understand these concepts before you move on to the walk-through.

Karma configuration

So far, the default Karma configuration has been used, but no explanation on the default configuration has been given yet. File watching is a useful default behavior that will now be reviewed.

File watching

File watching is enabled by default when the `karma init` command is used.
File watching in Karma is configured with the following definition in the
`karma.conf.js` file:

```
autoWatch: true,
```

The file watching feature works as expected and watches the files defined in the
configuration's `files` array. When a file is updated, changed, or deleted, Karma will
respond by rerunning the tests. From a TDD perspective, this is a great feature as
tests will continue to run without any manual intervention.

The main point to watch out for is the addition of files. If the file being added doesn't
match the criteria in the `files` array, the `autoWatch` parameter won't respond to the
change. As an example, let's consider that the files are defined as follows:

```
files : [ 'dir1/**/*.js']
```

If this is the case, the watcher will find all the files and subdirectory files ending in
`.js`. If a new file is in a different directory, not in `dir1`, then the watcher will not be
able to respond to the new file because it is in a different directory than what it was
configured in.

Using a bottom-up approach

The top-down approach of TDD can be very useful. It helps focus on user-facing
components first and then fills up the backend layer. One of the caveats to this
approach is that the specification being built is more user facing as opposed to it being
based on logic. The bottom-up approach builds from the inner components out to the
UI and the user. This kind of approach is extremely important when working with
complicated logic and requirements. With the bottom-up approach, you will first
build services, controllers, and directives with all the complexities using unit tests
and Karma. After this, you will expand to create end-to-end tests with Protractor.

Services

AngularJS services, factories, and resources are all important components.
Services are used to abstract application logic. They are used to provide single
responsibility for a particular action. Single responsibility allows components to
be easily tested and changed. This is because the focus is on one component and
not all the inner dependencies.

Here is a summary of some of the other AngularJS components that have been looked at so far:

- **Attributes and directives**: These drive actions and flow from the UI
- **Controllers**: This provides the glue between the UI and logic
- **Services**: This isolates the logic

Publishing and subscribing messages

One of the great features of AngularJS is its ability to publish and subscribe messages within a page. Publishing and subscribing messages is a powerful component, but like with anything, when used the wrong way, it can lead to a mess.

One area where this pattern is useful is when communicating across boundaries in an application. Application boundaries are important as they allow the UI to have isolated code. Complexity occurs when separate UI components need to be aware of changes in other areas of the UI. With a publishing and subscription model, applications can communicate seamlessly using messages. This chapter will focus on publishing and subscribing. You will be able to take a closer look at what boundaries are and determine good places to leverage this feature in your own applications.

There are two ways in which messages can be published. You can either emit or broadcast. It is important to know the difference as both work slightly differently, and they may affect the performance of your application.

Emitting

One way to publish events is to emit them. The documentation at `https://docs.angularjs.org/api/ng/type/$rootScope.Scope` gives the functionality of the `$emit()` method as follows:

> *Dispatches an event name upwards through the scope hierarchy notifying the registered $rootScope.Scope listeners.*

The important thing to note is `$emit()` notifies up through the scopes all the way to the top of the hierarchy. This is important because if you have an embedded controller scope, it is going to have to propagate all the way up to every controller and scope. This can cause a performance issue. Here is an example of how to emit an event:

```
$scope.someAction = function(){
  $scope.$emit('ANYEVENT');
};
```

The best way to see the upward propagation of the event is through a test. The next section will show you how to unit test the upward effect of `$emit()`.

Testing emit

The following tests have three controllers: `TopController`, `MiddleController`, and `BottomController`. `MiddleController` will emit the event. From this, an expectation can be made that `TopController` will receive the event and `BottomController` won't, as the emission propagates in an upward fashion. Here are the steps to test the `$emit()` method:

1. Create spies to test the emission of events:

   ```
   var topEventSpy = jasmine.createSpy();
   var bottomEventSpy = jasmine.createSpy();
   ```

2. The test setup first sets the hierarchy of scopes:

   ```
   inject(function($controller,$rootscope){
     var topScope = $rootscope.$new();
     var middleScope = topScope.$new();
     var bottomScope = middleScope.$new();
   ```

3. Then the controllers are set with their respective scopes:

   ```
   $controller('TopController',{$scope:topScope});
   $controller('MiddleController',{$scope:middleScope});
   $controller('BottomController',{$scope:bottomScope});
   ```

4. Set the spy to capture the events:

   ```
   topScope.$on('MIDDLEEMIT',topEventSpy);
   bottomScope.$on('MIDDLEEMIT',bottomEventSpy);
   ```

5. Emit the event from the middle scope:

   ```
   middleScope.$emit('MIDDLEEMIT');
   ```

6. Add the expectation that the top spy was called on the events:

   ```
   it('Should notify top controller',function(){
     expect(topEventSpy.wasCalled).toBe(true);
   });
   ```

7. Add the expectation that the bottom spy was not called:

   ```
   it('Should not notify bottom controller', function(){
     expect(bottomEventSpy.wasCalled).toBe(false);
   });
   ```

Here are a couple of things to note from the preceding test:

- This is a unit test that we will run in Karma.

- The `inject` method provides a reference to the `$controller` and `$rootscope` scopes. The `$rootscope` scope is the topmost scope of an AngularJS application. If you're using `$rootscope` to emit events, they wouldn't need to propagate anymore as `$rootscope` is at the highest level. In the later examples, `$rootscope` will be injected into the controller and used to listen to and send events.

- A scope can create a new child scope. A child scope is created using the `$new` method. You can imagine this to be equivalent to a page that has embedded containers:

```
<div ng-controller="topController"
  <div ng-controller="middleController">
    <div ng-controller="bottomController">
    </div>
  </div>
</div>
```

Testing broadcast

The documentation at `https://docs.angularjs.org/api/ng/type/$rootScope.Scope` states gives the functionality of the `$broadcast()` method as follows:

> *Dispatches an event name downwards to all child scopes (and their children) notifying the registered $rootScope.Scope listeners.*

As opposed to the `$emit` method, which pushes events up through the scope chain, `$broadcast` pushes events down the chain. The other important distinction to make is that the `$broadcast` event can't be cancelled, but `$emit` can be. These are small intricacies that if not understood properly can have a negative effect on the application. Like with the `$emit` event, the following example shows the way broadcasting works through a test.

Testing broadcast

Utilizing similar techniques from the emission test, here are the steps to test the broadcasting of events:

1. Create the spies:

```
var topEventSpy = jasmine.createSpy();
var bottomEventSpy = jasmine.createSpy();
```

2. Initialize the scopes:

```
var topScope = $rootScope.$new();
var middleScope = topScope.$new();
var bottomScope = middleScope.$new();
```

3. Set the respective controller scopes:

```
$controller('TopController',{$scope:topScope});
$controller('MiddleController',{$scope:middleScope});
$controller('BottomController',{$scope:bottomScope});
```

4. Set the spies to listen for the events:

```
topScope.$on('MIDDLEEMIT',topEventSpy);
bottomScope.$on('MIDDLEEMIT',bottomEventSpy);
```

5. Broadcast the event from `middleScope`:

```
middleScope.$broadcast('MIDDLEEMIT');
```

6. Have the expectation that the top scope was not touched:

```
it('Should not notify top controller',function(){
  expect(topEventSpy.wasCalled).toBe(false);
});
```

7. Have the expectation that the bottom scope received the message:

```
it('Should notify bottom controller', function(){
  expect(bottomEventSpy.wasCalled).toBe(true);
});
```

The preceding explanations have showed how to integrate and test two types of AngularJS events. As you progress through the rest of the event tests, you will find that the setup and techniques used here will be used throughout the rest of the chapter.

Publishing and subscribing – the good and bad

Knowing when to use publishing and subscribing is one thing, but knowing when *not* to use them is the difficult part.

The good

Before looking at the problems that publishing and subscribing can lead to, here are some of the best scenarios where you can use this technique:

- Communicating important events to different components of the application
- Reducing coupling

Communicating through events

When thinking about events that need to be coupled, it is important to think about what actions are driving the application. Given a bank application, events might be as simple as DEPOSITED and WITHDREW. These two simple events may be used in many other places. Think about you wanting to send an e-mail to the customer every time they withdrew or automatically updated some real-time report. Instead of polling the persistence layer, a real-time notification message can be used. In AngularJS, this means that the UI can be made up of different components that can respond to changes in one area, for example, UI notifications, updating workflows, enabling features, or anything you can think of.

Communicating events so that other components can respond to them is key. When you want to easily respond to events and changes, publishing and submitting is the way to go. The following is another test to show how communication can be used:

1. Create scopes for the controllers:

   ```
   recentTransactionScope = $rootScope.$new();
   atmScope = recentTransactionScope.$new();
   ```

2. Assign the scopes to the controllers:

   ```
   $controller('AtmController',{$scope:atmScope});
   $controller('RecentTransactionsController',
   {$scope:recentTransactionScope});
   ```

3. Set the spies:

   ```
   spyOn(atmScope,'$emit').and.callThrough();
   spyOn(recentTransactionScope.recent,'push');
   ```

4. Call the method being tested:

   ```
   atmScope.withdraw(3.33);
   ```

5. Set the expectation that the event was emitted:

   ```
   it('should emit an event',function(){
     expect(atmScope.$emit).toHaveBeenCalled();
   });
   ```

6. Set the expectation that the recent transactions received the event:

```
it('should send event to recent transactions',function(){
  expect(recentTransactionScope.recent.push).
  toHaveBeenCalled();
});
```

Here are the controllers to further clarify the code:

1. The `AtmController` property (publisher):

```
bankModule.controller('AtmController', ['$scope',
function($scope){
  $scope.withdraw = function(amount){
    $scope.$emit('WITHDREW',amount);
  }
}]);
```

2. The `RecentTransactionsController` property (subscriber):

```
bankModule.controller('RecentTransactionsController', ['$scope',
function($scope){
  $scope.recent = [];
  $scope.$on('WITHDREW',function(amount){
    $scope.recent.push(amount);
  })
}]);
```

As discussed with the tests, `AtmController` emits the `WITHDREW` event after a withdrawal occurs.

The preceding steps are just a simple example of how publishing and subscribing can help communicate important activities across your application.

Reducing coupling

Communication is one aspect of the benefits of publishing messages. Messaging gives you decreased coupling. Think about the preceding bank application that communicates when a withdrawal occurs. The messages may be used for many different aspects of the application, and since it is decoupled, we don't need to worry. If we think about it another way, the `withdraw` function doesn't care about the rest of the application. It only focuses on the fact that it will perform a withdrawal and then send a message upon its completion. From the subscription perspective, the recent transactions don't care where the withdrawal happens. It only has to focus on what it needs to do when this happens.

Decoupling the application can be extremely beneficial from a testing perspective. Take another look at the bank application if you want to refactor and separate out the tests. You could create a new test that is specific to the `RecentTransactions` property. Since the application is decoupled, it doesn't care about `AtmController`. The test can be separated out as follows:

1. The `beforeEach` function can be reduced to only deal with the scope of `recentTransactionsController` and `$rootScope`:

```
var recentTransactionScope = {};
var rootScope = {};
beforeEach(function(){
  module('bank');
  inject(function($controller,$rootScope){
    rootScope = $rootScope.$new();
    recentTransactionScope = $rootScope.$new();

    $controller('RecentTransactionsController',
    {$scope:recentTransactionScope});
  });
  spyOn(recentTransactionScope.recent,'push');
  rootScope.$emit('WITHDREW',3);
});
```

2. In the `beforeEach` function, add a spy to help with testing:

```
spyOn(recentTransactionScope.recent,'push');
```

3. Instead of calling the `AtmController` class's `withdraw` function, we can call `$emit` on `$rootScope`:

```
rootScope.$emit('WITHDREW',3);
```

4. The `afterEach` function and the expectation are the same as shown previously:

```
afterEach(function(){
  recentTransactionScope.recent.push.calls.reset();
  });
  it('should send event to recent transactions',function(){
    expect(recentTransactionScope.recent.push).
    toHaveBeenCalled();
});
```

This example has shown that using messaging, you can decouple tests. Decoupling application tests allows the application to grow without having to negatively refactor the entire application. In the preceding case, if `AtmController` is changed, the `recentTransactions` test and the `recentTransactions` controller won't need to be changed. As long as the `WITHDREW` event is published, `recentTransactions` will not have to be updated.

Harnessing the power of events

Publishing and subscribing events can lead to some ugly and hard-to-understand spaghetti code. Now that the foundations for the chapter have been reviewed, you can dive into implementing events into the search application.

The plan

The search application from *Chapter 5*, *Flip Flop*, is quite basic. At this point, it will return a set of results, and then when the user clicks on a result, details will appear. The application provides a foundation for future development. In this chapter, the functionality will be expanded to include publishing and subscribing. Here is the plan to expand the search application:

- The search application will be rebranded as a store application, and the search results will display a list of products.

- When a product is selected, details will be displayed.

- All selected products from the search will be available in a new view for "recently viewed" items.

- The detailed view of the product will have the option to "add to cart", and the product will then be available in the cart view.

The plan is somewhat ambitious, but with all the knowledge we have on TDD and AngularJS, the development should flow nicely.

Rebranding

The search application will be rebranded into a store application instead of rewriting the search functionality that has already been written. In order to leverage the existing search project, it will be copied into a new project file. Then, the new project will use the tests to drive the development changes and refactoring. The refactor steps have been left out, but a review of the code will show how the code and tests were modified to create the product application.

The refactor steps updated the unit tests and application to support the correct naming for the application. It is important to take away two things from this:

- Refactor small to introduce big changes. Small incremental changes help to progressively get to the next stage of the application. When big changes occur, it can be confusing to know where and what to change. With small changes, even though the same code is revisited several times, you can ensure the tests pass at each stage instead of ripping the application apart completely and then trying to put it all back together again.

- TDD applies during refactoring just as much as when doing core development. The refactor steps followed were the same as the TDD steps. Start with changing the test to meet our specification and then make the code run to meet the specification. Applying these principles helps keep productivity and focus.

Both the unit tests and end-to-end tests pass from the refactor steps. It is time to turn to the first feature of the application.

Seeing recently viewed items

Now that the initial refactoring is complete, the new functionality of the product application can be considered. The first specification that will be considered is the ability to see "recently viewed" items. The specification is broken down into two steps, as follows:

- The user selects a product to view the details
- They will be able to see the viewed products

This is an example of where broadcasting would be a good candidate. In the preceding case, the specification is concerned with when a product has been selected. In other words, when an event occurs, a subsequent action needs to happen. Using AngularJS events (`$broadcast()`/`$emit()`), the event of selecting a product to view can be published and then consumed by the recently viewed component.

The standard TDD life cycle will be used to build this component: test first, make it run, make it better. We will be using a bottom-up approach (unit test first). The main reason for choosing this approach is that there are multiple controllers involved, and it will be easier to start at the bottom and make our way up through the application.

Test first

The first test we will be writing is that the `SearchController` class will publish an event when a product is selected. The following sections detail how to write the test.

Assembling SearchController

Here are the steps to assemble the `SearchController` class:

1. Start with the test stub using the following code:

    ```
    describe('',function(){
      beforeEach(function(){
      });
      it(function(){
      });
    });
    ```

2. Get the scope of `SearchController` so that an action can be performed:

    ```
    describe('', function(){
      beforeEach(function(){
        module('product');
        inject(function($controller,$rootScope){
          var searchControllerScope = $rootScope.$new();
          $controller('SearchController',
          {$scope:searchControllerScope});
        });
      });
      it(function(){
      });
    });
    ```

3. Place a spy on the SELECTEDPRODUCT event:

    ```
    var selectedProductSpy = jasmine.createSpy();
    var searchControllerScope = {};
    beforeEach(function(){
      module('product');
      inject(function($controller,$rootScope){
        searchControllerScope = $rootScope.$new();
        $controller('SearchController',
    {$scope:searchControllerScope,$rootscope});
        searchControllerScope.$on('SELECTEDPRODUCT',
        selectedProductSpy);
      });
    })
    ```

4. Add a cleanup function to clear the scope after each test and clear the spy:

    ```
    afterEach(function(){
      searchControllerScope = {};
      selectedProductSpy.reset();
    });
    ```

Selecting a product

The test requires that a SELECTEDPRODUCT event has been published. The event will occur when the selected product method is called with `productId`:

```
var fakeProduct = {productId:1};
searchControllerScope.selectProduct(fakeProduct);
```

Expecting events to be published

The expectation is that `selectedProductSpy` has been called:

```
it('',function(){
  expect(selectedProductSpy).toHaveBeenCalled();
});
```

Making the search controller run

Now we have to make the test pass and run. Here are the steps:

1. Start Karma using the following command:

    $karma start

2. You'll get an error, namely `TypeError: 'undefined' is not a function (evaluating 'searchControllerScope.selectProduct(fakeProduct)')`. To rectify this, perform the following step:

    1. Add the method to `SearchController`:

        ```
        $scope.selectProduct = function(){};
        ```

3. Then you'll get the error `Expected spy unknown to have been called. Error: Expected spy unknown to have been called`. To rectify this, perform the following steps:

    1. The expectation has failed, which means the spy was never called. Open up `SearchController` and add functionality to the `selectProduct` method to emit an event:

        ```
        $scope.selectProduct = function(productId){
          $rootScope.$broadcast('SELECTEDPRODUCT',productId);
        };
        ```

    2. Rerun the test.

4. The test will pass.

Now when a product is selected, the event is broadcasted. Any function wanting to know when something gets selected can simply listen for the broadcast.

Recently viewed unit test

The next step is to add another test from the subscription side of the event to `RecentlyViewedController`.

Test first

Again, the walk-through of the test steps will use the 3 A's.

Assembling RecentlyViewedController

Here are the steps to assemble `RecentlyViewedController`:

1. Start with the test stub using the following code:

```
describe('',function(){
  beforeEach(function(){
  });
  it(function(){
  });
});
```

2. Get the scope of `RecentlyViewedController` so that an action can be performed:

```
describe('',function(){
  beforeEach(function(){
    module('product');
    inject(function($controller, $rootScope){
      var recentlyViewedScope = $rootScope.$new();
      $controller('RecentlyViewedController',
      {$scope:recentlyViewedScope});
    });
  });
  it(function(){
  });
});
```

3. Confirm that the number of recently viewed products is equal to `0`:

```
expect(recentlyViewedScope.recent.length).toBe(0);
```

Invoking a recently viewed item

The action for this test is that the SELECTEDPRODUCT event has been published. Now add the publish event:

```
var fakeProductEvent = {productId:1};
$rootscope.$broadcast('SELECTEDPRODUCT',fakeProductEvent);
```

Confirming RecentlyViewedController

The assertion is that the number of recently viewed products is now equal to 1:

```
it('',function(){
  expect(recentlyViewedScope.recent.length).toBe(1);
});
```

Making RecentlyViewedController run

Here are the steps to run `RecentlyViewedController`:

1. Start Karma using the following command:

    ```
    $ karma start
    ```

2. You'll get an error, namely `Error: [ng:areq] Argument 'RecentlyViewedController' is not a function, got undefined`. To rectify this error, perform the following steps:

    1. Create the required controller and create a new file named `RecentlyViewedController.js`.

    2. Then, add the following details:

        ```
        angular.module('product')
        .controller('RecentlyViewedController',['$scope',
        function($scope){
        }]);
        ```

    3. Rerun the test.

3. Then you'll get the error `TypeError: 'undefined' is not an object (evaluating 'recentlyViewedScope recent.length')`, which means that the first expectation, that is the recent product 0, has been hit. As the object is undefined, add it to the `recentlyViewedScope` scope.

4. Then you'll get the error `Expected 0 to be 1. Error: Expected 0 to be 1`. To rectify this, perform the following steps:

    1. The expectation has been hit. Now the behavior of the event needs to be added to the controller.

    2. Add `$rootScope` to the controller:

        ```
        .controller('RecentlyViewedController',['$scope',
        '$rootScope',function($scope,$rootScope){
        ```

    3. Subscribe to the event from `$rootScope`:

        ```
        $rootScope.$on('SELECTEDPRODUCT',function(productEvent){
        })
        ```

4. Now add `productEvent` to the recent array:

    ```
    $rootScope.$scope.recent.push(productEvent)
    ```

5. Rerun the test.

5. The tests will now pass.

End-to-end testing

The unit tests are complete and will verify that the publisher and subscriber can both communicate with events. Now the walk-through will look at the application as a whole and will show you how to create an end-to-end test. The specification for recently viewed items is that in a given search result:

*   A product is selected
*   It will be available in the recently viewed items

Now, it is time to move on to actually creating the test.

Test first

As always, start by translating the specification in the test using the 3 A's, as the tests will utilize the existing tests.

Assembling the recently viewed end-to-end test

Before you repeat the code from *Chapter 5, Flip Flop*, you should notice that the first test already searches for and retrieves the search results. Therefore, the recently viewed test can be embedded within the existing test for a search result that is already available. At the bottom of the existing function of a search query, initialize the test stub:

```
describe('when I type in a search query', function(){
// ...
describe('',function(){
  beforeEach(function(){
     });
     it('',function(){
  });
});
```

There is nothing else to assemble for the test, and you can move on to the next step.

Selecting a search result

Now, `searchResult` needs to be invoked using the following steps:

1. The first step will be to select the first `searchResult` element:

   ```
   var firstResult = searchResult.first();
   ```

2. Find the link within the first item:

   ```
   var resultLink = firstResult.element(by.css('a'));
   ```

3. Click on the result:

   ```
   resultLink.click();
   ```

Confirming recently viewed items

Now that a product has been selected and one product has been added to the recently viewed items list, we need to view the recently viewed items. Here are the steps to do this:

1. Get the recently viewed items:

   ```
   var recentlyViewedItems = element(by.repeater
   ('items in recent'));
   ```

2. Confirm that the count of recently viewed items is equal to 0:

   ```
   expect(recentlyViewedItems.count()).toBe(1);
   ```

Making the recentlyViewedItems test pass

Now the test needs to pass. Here are the steps to do this:

1. Start the website:

   ./node_modules/http_server/bin/http_server

2. Run Protractor:

   ./node_modules/protractor/bin/protractor chromeOnlyConf.js

3. You'll get an error, namely `Expected 0 to be 1.`.

4. The error is that the expectation has failed. It is time to add the controller and repeater to the recently viewed items list to show the items:

   ```
   <div ng-controller="RecentlyViewedController">
     <div ng-repeat="item in recent">
       {{item}}
     </div>
   </div>
   ```

5. Rerun the test

6. The error is the same as before. This time, Protractor errors don't give any clues to what the issue is. The next step is to open up a browser and see what the web browser JavaScript console is saying. Point your browser to `http://localhost:8080/#/recentlyViewed`. Immediately, one error will be visible, namely `[ng:areq] Argument 'RecentlyViewedController' is not a function, got undefined`. To rectify this, perform the following steps:

    1. Now that there is an actual error to fix, progress can be made. The error indicates that the controller was not available. As the controller has not been added, it is time to add the controller to the page. Open up the `index.html` page and add the controller reference:

       ```
       <script src="app/recentlyViewedController.js"></script>
       ```

    2. Rerun the test.

7. Now the test will be successful.

Making recently viewed items better

The recently viewed controller is now complete. It would be nice to better organize the view, however this can happen later. The point of this exercise was to establish communication between separate views and create a usable function. This has been achieved, and now you can move to the next step of the walk-through.

Creating a product cart

Another important aspect of the application is the ability to add products to a cart. A publishing and subscription model will be used to publish when an item has been saved to a cart. A subscription to the event will then keep track of items in the cart so the user can easily see when saved items get updated in real time. Here is the specification given the product details of a particular product:

- If the product is saved to a cart
- Product will be displayed in the product cart view

Now the necessary things are in order to get down to the 3 A's.

Publisher test first

The publisher will come from `searchDetailController`. The test will need to ensure that when an item is saved, an event is published.

Assembling searchDetailController

The `searchDetailController` already has some unit tests written. The existing test can be leveraged to confirm the publishing feature. Here are the steps to create a subtest to handle the saving of a cart:

1. Start with an inner stub:

    ```
    describe('',function(){
      beforeEach(function(){
      });
      it('',function(){
      });
    })
    ```

2. In order to test that an event has been emitted, a spy will be needed on `$rootScope`. Bring in `$rootScope` and add a spy to it:

    ```
    // ...
    var savedToCartEventSpy = jasmine.createSpy();
    beforeEach(function(){
      inject(function($rootScope){
        $rootScope.$on('SAVEDTOCART',savedToCartEventSpy);
      });
    });
    ```

3. Add `afterEach` to reset the spy:

    ```
    afterEach(function(){
      savedToCartEventSpy.calls.reset();
    });
    ```

Invoking the saving of a product

In the `beforeEach` section, select the method and make the following changes:

```
beforeEach(function(){
  // ...
  var fakeProduct = {productId:1};
  searchDetailScope.saveProduct(fakeProduct);
})
```

Confirming the save event

The expectation is that the spy has been called:

```
it('',function(){
  expect(savedToCartEventSpy).toHaveBeenCalled();
})
```

Making the saveProduct test pass

Now we need to make the test pass. Here are the steps to make the `saveProduct` test pass:

1. Start Karma:

   ```
   $ karma start
   ```

2. The first error will be `TypeError: 'undefined' is not a function (evaluating 'searchDetailScope.saveProduct(fakeProduct)')`. If you get this error, then follow these steps:

   1. The function doesn't exist on the scope. Add it using the following code:

      ```
      $scope.saveProduct = function(product){};
      ```

   2. Rerun the test.

3. Now the error has hit the expectation and says `Expected spy unknown to have been called`. In this case, follow the given steps:

   1. The smallest thing we can add to the test is the ability to emit the event from the method. First add `$rootScope` to the controller:

      ```
      .controller('SearchDetailController', ['$scope',
      '$routeParams', 'productService', '$rootScope',
      function($scope, $routeParams, productService, $rootScope){
      ```

   2. Then add the `Sbroadcast()` event to it:

      ```
      $rootScope.$broadcast('SAVEDTOCART', product);
      ```

   3. Rerun the test.

4. The test is successful.

Test for the subscriber first

The subscriber unit test will confirm that when a SAVEDTOCART event is emitted, then the product will be added to the cart object. The specification is as a SAVEDTOCART event is given, the following action will be performed:

- It will add the product to the cart

Assembling the product cart test

Here are the steps to assemble the product cart test:

1. Create a new file, `spec/unit/cart.js`.

2. Start with the base stub:

```
describe('', function(){
  beforeEach(function(){
  });
  it('', function(){
  });
});
```

3. Initialize the module:

```
module('product');
```

4. Initialize the scope so that expectations can be made:

```
var scope = {};
beforeEach(function(){
  // ...
  inject(function($controller){
    $controller('CartController',{$scope:scope});
  });
});
```

5. Initialize `$rootScope` so subscriptions can be made:

```
inject(function($controller,$rootScope){
  scope = $rootScope.$new();
  $controller('CartController',{$scope:scope,
  $rootScope:$rootScope});
  });
```

6. The last thing to confirm is that the cart is empty. Add the following expectation to ensure the test is set up properly:

```
expect(scope.cart.length).toBe(0);
```

Invoking a saved cart event

This test is around the fact that when the SAVEDTOCART event is published, the CartController property will perform a specific action. Add the publishing of the event to the `beforeEach` method:

```
beforeEach(function(){
  // ...
  var fakeProduct = {productId:1};
  $rootScope.$broadcast('SAVEDTOCART',fakeProduct);
});
```

Confirming the saved cart

Now that the test has been set up and the act performed, you can assert. Assert that the number of cart items is equal to 1 by adding the following code:

```
it('',function(){
  expect(scope.cart.length).toBe(1);
});
```

Making the cart controller test run

Now it's time to walk the test through the cycle by following the given steps until we get a green test:

1. Start Karma:

   ```
   $ karma start
   ```

2. The first error is `Error: [ng:areq] Argument 'CartController' is not a function, got undefined`. As seen previously, the controller hasn't been created. Create a new file and set up a stub controller (`/app/cart.js`):

   ```
   angular.module('product')
   .controller('CartController', ['$scope',function($scope){
   }]);
   ```

3. The next error will be `TypeError: 'undefined' is not an object (evaluating 'scope.cart.length')`. This indicates that no object was found on the scope named `cart`. Go ahead and create it now in `app/cart.js`:

   ```
   $scope.cart = [];
   ```

4. Then, you'll get an expectation error, namely `Expected 0 to be 1. Error: Expected 0 to be 1`. To rectify this, perform the following steps:

   1. At this point, the controller is not doing anything with the event being emitted. Add `$rootScope` as a dependency to the application:

      ```
      .controller('CartController', ['$scope','$rootScope',
      function($scope,$rootScope){
      ```

   2. Add the handling logic to capture the event and add the product to the cart:

      ```
      $rootScope.$on('SAVEDTOCART',function(productEvent){
        $scope.cart.push(productEvent);
      });
      ```

5. Success! All the tests have passed.

End-to-end testing

The unit tests are now complete, and it is now time to perform end-to-end testing for the cart.

Assembling the cart's end-to-end test

The test comes from the perspective of being on a product detail view and selecting a **Save to Cart** button. Once the item has been saved, it should be available in the cart view. Here are the steps to assemble the cart's end-to-end test:

1. Create a new file named `spec/e2e/cartScenario.js`.

2. Start with the base template test:

```
describe('',function(){
  beforeEach(function(){
  });
  it('',function(){
  });
});
```

3. The next thing we need to do is navigate to a product page:

```
browser.get("#/product/1");
```

4. Select the button that will save the cart:

```
var saveToCartButton = element(by.buttonText
('Save to Cart'));
```

Invoking a save to cart action

The action is to click on the **Save** button using the following code:

```
saveToCartButton.click();
```

Confirming products have been saved

The assert is to confirm that the cart view now has at least one product:

```
it('',function(){
  var productsInCart = element.all(by.repeater
('product in cart'));
  expect(productsInCart.count()).toBe(1);
})
```

Making the cart's end-to-end test pass

Here is the walk-through of the process of making the application run:

1. Start the site:

    ```
    $ ./node_modules/http-server/bin/http-server .
    ```

2. Run Protractor:

    ```
    $ ./node_modules/protractor/bin/protractor chromeOnlyConf.js
    ```

3. The first error is `NoSuchElementError: No element found using locator: by.buttonText("Save to Cart")`. To rectify this, perform the following steps:

    1. Go ahead and create the button within the product detail's `app/searchDetail.html` partial view:

        ```
        <button>Save to Cart</button>
        ```

    2. Rerun the test.

4. The next error is `Expected 0 to be 1`. To rectify this, perform the following steps:

    1. This error means that the count is `0` for products in the cart. By reviewing the index page, you can see that the cart doesn't even exist in the page. First, add a reference to the cart controller:

        ```
        <script src="app/cart.js"></script>
        ```

    2. Next, the items in the cart need to be added to the page. First, add a tag with the controller:

        ```
        <div ng-controller="CartController"></div>
        ```

    3. Finally, add a repeater to display the product in the cart:

        ```
        <ul>
          <li ng-repeat="product in cart">{{product}}</li>
        </ul>
        ```

    4. Rerun the test.

5. The same error occurs, `Expected 0 to be 1`. To rectify this, perform the following steps:

    1. Even though the product data has been added, the test is still failing. The next question is whether anything is being added to the cart. In this case, no. The button is being selected but no action has been associated with it. Update the button in `app/searchDetail.html` to use the `searchDetailController` class's `saveProduct` method:

       ```
       <button ng-click="saveProduct()">Save to Cart</button>
       ```

    2. Rerun the test.

6. All the tests pass.

Self-test questions

The following are some questions to check your understanding:

Q1. When broadcasting a message, it propagates up the scope's hierarchy.

   1. True
   2. False

Q2. The following creates a spy in Jasmine:

   1. `var spy = jasmine.createSpy();`
   2. `var spy = jasmine.$new();`
   3. `var spy = jasmine.createFake();`

Q3. The `$rootScope` scope is the highest level scope in AngularJS.

   1. True
   2. False

Additionally, if you want more practice, add the ability to add likes to the page.

Summary

This chapter has explored events within AngularJS. You saw two types of AngularJS event emitters: `$broadcast()` and `$emit()`. You also saw some examples of applying TDD to events and how events give a separation of controllers and code. In addition, you expanded the types of testing techniques to include services and reiterated the testing of controllers and models. You also explored further configuration of Karma to use its features. In the next chapter, you will look at the integration and testing of data and APIs into an AngularJS application.

7
Give Me Some Data

Applications need a way to consume the ever-expansive world of data. Most applications written today consume data. Luckily for AngularJS developers, consuming data is quite easy. Testing data consumption is also a core component of the framework. In this chapter, we will cover the following topics:

- Integrating a REST-based service
- Creating and mocking AngularJS's `$http`
- Handling exceptions
- Implementing a fake API builder pattern

REST – the language of the Web

Representational State Transfer (**REST**) defines how the Web should communicate. From an AngularJS application standpoint, the main concern is with the HTTP methods. For HTTP methods, REST can be thought of as the verbs or actions that an HTTP request can make. Specifically, an HTTP request can make these request types: GET, POST, PUT, and DELETE. From an API standpoint, the HTTP methods can be used to determine how logic should handle the specific HTTP request type. Here is a further look at the common HTTP methods:

HTTP Method	Description	Example
GET	Retrieves data from an endpoint	`curl --request GET 'http://<SOME URL>'`
POST	Posts a new data element to the endpoint	`curl -request POST 'http://<SOME URL>' -data 'anydata'`

HTTP Method	Description	Example
PUT	Inserts or updates the enclosed data element to the endpoint	`curl -request POST 'http://<SOME URL>' -data 'anydata'`
DELETE	Deletes a request to the endpoint	`curl --request DELETE 'http://<SOME URL>'`

> The `curl` tool is a command-line tool that can be used to make requests. On Unix machines, it is available in the command line by simply typing `curl`. For Windows machines, it is best to install Git bash and access it through the Git bash command line. Installation instructions for Git and Git bash can be found at `http://git-scm.com/downloads`.

As can be seen from the preceding explanation, the RESTful components of HTTP can define the basics for most APIs. The preceding REST approach is different from other web service techniques or protocols and can be used by practically anything. For their simplicity, REST-based web services are the best options. In this chapter, the focus will only be on how to use AngularJS with a REST-based API.

Getting started with REST

Before jumping into how AngularJS communicates with a REST layer, it is important to see how to communicate using standard tools within a browser. As you saw from the previous definition, `curl` can be used to communicate to a REST API. Although making a manual HTTP request outside of a browser is useful, you also need to understand the basics of how a browser makes an API request without a framework. In a browser, requests can be made to REST layers through asynchronous calls. This allows requests that won't affect the other parts of the application to be made; that is, the page won't freeze and become unusable. The web page remains useable while the request is made.

Browsers provide a mechanism to make asynchronous REST calls using an XMLHttpRequest method. An XMLHttpRequest method can be used to make an HTTP GET, POST, PUT, or DELETE request. Here is an example of how to make a GET request:

```
var request = new XMLHttpRequest();
request.open('GET', '/any/rest/endpoint');
request.send();
```

The preceding example creates a new request, specifies the request type and location, and finally, sends the request. The missing piece is the handling of the response. Add the following code just before the send method:

```
request.onreadstatechange = function(){
  if (request.readyState === 4) {
    console.log('received response with status: '+request.status);
  }
};
```

The preceding code handles when the request has received a response from the server and is complete (readystate === 4). Within the condition given in the code, you can handle the parsing of the response, the determining status of the request, and so on.

What's great about the preceding code is that it doesn't require a framework. The problem is that the code can grow in size and become repetitive for every request. AngularJS has abstracted the request for you.

Testing asynchronous calls

Now that you understand how to make HTTP requests through the browser, we need to understand how to test these calls. The preceding requests are asynchronous. Asynchronous means there is no guarantee of when the function will complete. For your reference, here is an example of synchronous sequential logic:

```
var synchronousFunc = function(){
  console.log('In synchronousFunc');
};
synchronousFunc();
console.log('After call to synchronousFunc');
```

When the preceding code is run, the output is as follows:

In synchronousFunc

After call to synchronousFunc

Each function call occurs in the order of the call. With an asynchronous request, the order is not guaranteed. A callback function is passed into a function to inform you when a method is complete.

> Callback functions have two main conventions. The first is the jQuery-based method. The second is the Node.js method. The jQuery convention uses two callbacks as the last arguments to a method. The first callback is for success, and the second is for an error. The Node.js convention is to use a single callback as the last argument. The callback has two parameters, the first being an error and the second being the successful result.
>
> It is up to you to decide which convention to use based on what you're developing for. Don't create your own new convention; use one of the preceding conventions so that other developers can easily understand and read your code.

Here is an example of the output of an asynchronous method:

```
var asynchronousFunc = function(callback){
  setTimeout(callback,0);
};
var callback = function(){
  console.log('In asynchronousFunc');
};
asynchronousFunc(callback);
console.log('After call to asynchronousFunc');
```

When the preceding code is run, the output is as follows:

```
After call to asynchronousFunc

In asynchronousFunc
```

The next sections will look at how test to asynchronous functions in Karma and Protractor.

Creating asynchronous calls in Karma

From the preceding asynchronous example, it should be clear that the way in which you test needs to be modified to account for asynchronous behavior. Luckily, this is fairly straightforward when testing with Karma.

Here are the steps to test the preceding asynchronous method using Karma:

1. Create the stub test using the following code:

```
describe('',function(){
  beforeEach(function(){
  });
  it('',function(){
  });
});
```

2. Create a spy to test when the asynchronous method gets called:

```
var spy = jasmine.createSpy();
```

3. Call the asynchronous method in the `beforeEach` function:

```
beforeEach(function(){
  var asynchronousFunc = function(callback){
    setTimeout(callback,0);
  };
  var callback = function(){
    spy();
  };
  asynchronousFunc(callback);
});
```

4. Add a callback to the parameters of the `beforeEach` function. By doing this, you have made the function asynchronous:

```
beforeEach(function(done){
  ...
});
```

5. Call the `done` method in the `asynchronousFunc` callback:

```
var callback = function(){
  spy();
  done();
};
```

6. Add the assertion function:

```
it('',function(){
  expect(spy).toHaveBeenCalled();
});
```

The key to the preceding code is that a callback was passed into the `beforeEach` function. You can try to run this test without the callback and see whether the test will fail. A callback can be passed into the `beforeEach`, `afterEach`, `describe`, and `it` methods.

You will be leveraging this example through the rest of the chapter, so be sure that you understand the main concepts. Now that you have tested in Karma, the next section will show you what Protractor offers from an asynchronous standpoint.

Creating asynchronous calls in Protractor

Protractor is different in the way it handles asynchronous actions. It has been optimized to handle asynchronous actions, specifically, promises. As an example, when a test navigates to a page, Protractor will wait until AngularJS has been loaded until it starts running the tests. Julie Ralph, the main contributor and creator of Protractor, sums it up in this GitHub issue (`https://github.com/angular/protractor/issues/716`):

> *Protractor patches Jasmine so that it is automatically asynchronous, and a test case finishes when the WebDriver queue of commands is finished.*

What this means is that you don't have to think about how the calls are being rendered and when the promises are complete. It even waits for `$http` requests to complete. Here is an example of using Protractor:

```
describe('When I type in a search query', function(){
  var searchResult = element.all(by.repeater("result in results"));
  beforeEach(function(){
    browser.get("/index.html");
    $('input').sendKeys('any value');
    element(by.buttonText('search')).searchButton.click();
  });
  it('Should then add the result', function(){
    expect(searchResult.count()).toBe(1);
  });
});
```

The preceding code snippet is taken from *Chapter 6, Tell the World*. It highlights how Protractor executes each one of the commands and takes care of the asynchronous behaviors for you. In the next section, you will see how to make REST requests using AngularJS.

Making REST requests using AngularJS

Now that we have looked at what REST requests are and seen how to test asynchronously in Karma and Protractor, it is time to see how to make a request in AngularJS. At the lowest level, AngularJS provides the $http module. The module allows you to make HTTP requests. By visiting the documentation (`https://docs.angularjs.org/api/ng/service/$http`), we can see that it says the following:

> *The $http service is a core Angular service that facilitates communication with the remote HTTP servers via the browser's XMLHttpRequest object.*

As you have already seen how to make an XMLHttpRequest, you should feel at ease that you know what is going on under the hood. Here is a simple example of how to make an $http.get request in AngularJS:

```
$http.get('/any/rest/endpoint')
  .success(function(data,status,header,config){
  });
  .error(function(data,status,header,config){
  });
```

The success/error function is called asynchronously once the request is complete.

Using $http is not the only way to make a request. If an API is completely REST-based, AngularJS provides the $resource module. A resource gets defined and used as shown in the following steps:

1. Define a resource for a specific end point:

   ```
   var thing = $resource('/any/rest/endpoint/:id',
   {id: '@id'});
   ```

2. Make the HTTP GET request:

   ```
   thing.get({id:1},function(aThing){
     ...
   });
   ```

The preceding example defines a resource that retrieves aThing based on an ID. It then retrieves that data with a GET request.

Both of the preceding examples show you how to create requests in AngularJS. You will be looking at the $http method in the remaining examples, but it is good to understand the different ways in which requests can be created in AngularJS.

Testing with AngularJS REST

Now that you have seen how to make requests in AngularJS and how to test asynchronously, you will need to look at how to put it together. The following example looks at a specific service and then discusses how to test using Karma.

Testing the product service

The service that needs to be tested is as follows:

```
angular.module('anyModule')
  .service('productService', ['$http', function($http){
    return {
      search: function(query){
        return $http.get('/product/search');
      }
    };
  });
```

The preceding `productService` parameter provides an object search that takes in a query and returns a `$http` promise. The product service can be used in a controller as follows:

```
productService.search(query)
  .success(function(data){
    $scope.result = data;
  })
  .error(function(data){
    $scope.error = data;
  });

angular.module('anyModule')
  .controller('productController',['$scope','productService',
function($scope,productService){
    $scope.search = function(query){
productService.search(query)
      .success(function(data){
        $scope.result = data;
      })
      .error(function(data){
        $scope.error = data;
      });
    }]);
```

The preceding use of the `productService` shows you that because an `$http` promise is returned, you can use the `success` and `error` functions to define what needs to occur after. Now that there is a controller and a service, the next section will show you how to test the components.

Testing $http with Karma

The Karma test will look to confirm the behavior of `productService` if the `$http` call is successful and is one to look at if an error occurs. The main difference between this test and others that have been looked at so far is that you are creating a request to something outside of AngularJS. This is a perfect case of use mocking. You can set up a fake object around `$http` to test the `success` and `error` paths of the request. AngularJS provides a mock object that can be used, which is Angular mock's `$httpBackend`.

Here are the steps to create a positive test — when the request is successful:

1. Start with the test stub:

   ```
   describe('',function(){
     beforeEach(function(){
     });
   it('',function(){
   });
   });
   ```

2. Initialize the module:

   ```
   beforeEach(function(){
     module('anyModule');
   });
   ```

3. Inject `$httpBackend` and `productService` in the `beforeEach` function:

   ```
   var $httpBackend = null;
   var productService = null;
   beforeEach(function(){
     module('anyModule');
   inject(function(_$httpBackend_,_productService_){
       $httpBackend = _$httpBackend_;
       productService = _productService_;
     });
   });
   ```

4. Mock the GET successful request with an HTTP status code of 200 as follows:

```
it('',function(){
  $httpBackend.when('GET','/product/search').respond(200,'');
});
```

5. Set the expectation as follows:

```
it('',function(){
  ...
  $httpBackend.expectGET('/product/search');
});
```

6. Make the call to productService using the following code:

```
productService.search('any');
```

7. Flush the request using the following code:

```
$httpBackend.flush();
```

As you can see, $httpBackend allows expectations and mock responses to be controlled. To tie up loose ends, here are the additional expectations for a failed request. Follow the steps to add expectations for a failed request:

1. Add the expectation stub to an asynchronous parameter:

```
it('',function(done){
});
```

2. Mock the GET unsuccessful request with an HTTP status code of 500:

```
$httpBackend.when('GET','/product/search').respond(500,'');
```

3. Call productService.Search:

```
productService.search('any');
```

4. Confirm that the error function gets called:

```
productService.search('any').error(function(){
  expect(true).toBe(true);
  done();
});
```

5. Flush the request:

```
$httpBackend.flush();
```

We have not added any other layers to the application and are able to confirm how it will work during a successful and unsuccessful request. In the next section, you will see how to test HTTP requests in Protractor.

Mocking requests with Protractor

Now that unit tests for the backend are complete, you can move to the frontend and test an HTTP request through Protractor. You might not always want to do this. Protractor is supposed to test your site from an end-to-end perspective. This means that all layers of the application will be touched. One benefit of the following example is that it will help in cases where you haven't set up the backend rest service. You can begin by laying out the page and interactions before the backend is complete. This can help when you're just putting your site together.

In order to mock the backend HTTP layer for Protractor, we will use $httpBackend, which is part of the ngMockE2E module and is used to mock the backend HTTP layer for Protractor. The $httpBackend property used for Protractor is different from the one used in the previous Karma test. To use end-to-end $httpBackend you will need to inject ngMockE2E as a dependency into the application. For this reason, it is not a viable solution to have in a production site.

Here are the steps that are to be mocked using $httpBackend in Protractor:

1. Add AngularJS and Angular mocks to the web page:

   ```
   <script src="bower_components/angular/angular.js"></script>
   <script src="bower_components/angular-mocks/
   angular-mocks.js"></script>
   ```

2. Create a module and require ngMockE2E:

   ```
   angular.module('anyModule', ['ngMockE2E'])
   ```

3. Add a run function that uses $httpBackend:

   ```
   .run(['$httpBackend',function($httpBackend) {
   ```

4. Create the mock data:

   ```
   .run(['$httpBackend',function($httpBackend) {
   var products = [{id: 'id1',name:'product1'}, {id:
   'id2',name:'product2'}];
   }]);
   ```

5. Set the mock data request:

   ```
   .run(['$httpBackend',function($httpBackend) {
   var products = [{id: 'id1',name:'product1'}, {id:
   'id2',name:'product2'}];
   $httpBackend.whenGET('/product/search').respond(products);
   }]);
   ```

Now the request to `/product/search` will respond with the products defined in the mock. This means that the application will work without the need for a backend service and will be able to be tested as an application with a backend service. A complete example using a mocked backend will be shown in the walk-through.

Displaying products with REST

All the core components of REST, asynchronous testing, and mocking HTTP requests have been discussed. Now, the following walk-through will provide a full example that will look at displaying products that are retrieved through an external service. The example will ignore the creation of an external service and focus on the data it provides: a list of products in a JSON format. The walk-through will take a bottom-up approach so that the core data layer is worked out before adding the UI elements.

Unit testing product requests

The approach from the unit level is to create a service to manage the HTTP requests for products. The controller will then be built up the same way.

Setting up the project

Before writing tests, the project needs to have a structure. Here is what the initial project structure looks like:

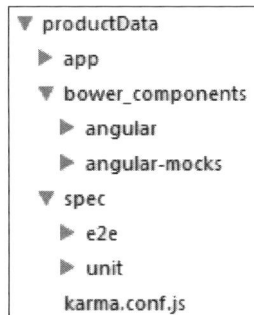

```
▼ productData
    ▶ app
    ▼ bower_components
        ▶ angular
        ▶ angular-mocks
    ▼ spec
        ▶ e2e
        ▶ unit
    karma.conf.js
```

Karma configuration

Now that the project template has been set up, a couple of adjustments need to be made. The Karma configuration needs to use a headless browser and set up the test files to the correct location. Open up `karma.conf.js` and make the following changes:

1. Update the `browsers` section to PhantomJS for headless browser testing:

   ```
   browsers: ['PhantomJS'],
   ```

2. Update the `files` section to include the unit test folders:

   ```
       files: [
   'bower_components/angular/angular.js',
           'bower_components/angular-mocks/angular-mocks.js',
   'app/**/*.js',
           'spec/unit/**/*.js'
       ],
   ```

Karma has been configured and the project template has been created. The next step is to set up an API builder for the product data. This will allow for a consistent interface to be used in a test where mocking data is required.

Using an API builder pattern

A builder is an object that is used to create another object; it will be used to create test data. An API builder can reduce duplication and the time taken to create tests. It provides a central way to handle methods and create data. If a builder is not used, then every test written will have to have a separate distinct way of creating data. This is an especially bad design when the API being used changes!

The product data API is defined by a single route/products. The expected response is a list of products. Here are the steps to create a builder for the product API:

1. Create a new file in the `spec` folder named `productDataBuilder.js`:

   $ touch productDataBuilder.js

2. Create a new function named `productDataBuilder`:

   ```
   module.exports = function productDataBuilder() {};
   ```

3. Return an object with methods to set IDs, names, and to actually build an object:

   ```
   module.exports = function productDataBuilder() {
       return {
   ```

```
            withId: function (id) {
            },
            withName: function (name) {
            },
            build: function () {
            }
        };
    };
```

4. Initialize a basic product:

```
module.exports = function productDataBuilder() {
    return {
        _mockProduct: { id: 1, name: 'productName' },
        withId: function (id) {
        },
        withName: function (name) {
        },
        build: function () {
        }
    };
};
```

5. Have the setter commands update the mock product:

```
return {
    ...
withId: function (id) {
    this._mockProduct.id = id;
        return this;
    },
    withName: function (name) {
        this._mockProduct.name = name;
        return this;
    },
};
```

6. Have the build method return the mock data:

```
return {
build: function () {
    return this._mockProduct;
    }
};
```

The builder allows you to use a fluent interface to create products. The simplest use is as follows:

```
var productDataBuilder = require('../productDataBuilder');
var someProduct = productDataBuilder.build();
```

A more complicated use will be to set the ID and name to something such as the following:

```
var productDataBuilder = require('../productDataBuilder');
var someProduct = productDataBuilder.withId(9999)
.withName('Product 9999');
```

The preceding `productDataBuilder` object will be used in the Karma test.

The product data service

It's time to get to the actual test. The same TDD life cycle that has been used throughout the book will be used; test first, make it run, and make it better. As the creation and testing of a service that uses HTTP has already been discussed, this walk-through will be skipped. For reference, the tests are in the code repository and the service is defined as follows:

```
angular.module('product')
  .service('productService', ['$http',function($http){
    return {
      getAll : function(){
        return $http.get('/products')
      }
    };
  }]);
```

With the service complete, the next step is to look at the controller and how to actually make use of the HTTP data.

The product data controller

The next component needed is a controller so that the UI can use `productService`. The controller needs to have one method to make the request for products. In the method, it needs to set `$result` when the request is successful and `$error` when the request is unsuccessful.

Assembling the product controller test

Here are the steps to assemble the product controller:

1. Create a new test file for the product controller `spec/productController.js`:

    ```
    $ touch spec/productController.js
    ```

2. Use the standard test stub:

    ```
    describe('',function(){
      beforeEach(function(){
      });
      it(function(){
      });
    });
    ```

3. Create variables for `scope` and `$httpBackend`:

    ```
    var scope = {};
    var $httpBackend = null;
    ```

4. Initialize the product module:

    ```
    beforeEach(function(){
      module('product');
    });
    ```

5. Get the `$controller` and `$httpBackend`:

    ```
    beforeEach(function(){
      inject(function($controller,_$htttpBackend_){
      });
    });
    ```

6. Set `$httpBackend` to the injected variable:

    ```
    inject(function($controller,_$httpBackend_){
    $httpBackend = _$httpBackend_;
    ```

7. Initialize the controller scope:

    ```
    inject(function($controller,_$httpBackend_){
    $httpBackend = _$httpBackend_;
    $controller('ProductController',{$scope:scope});
    ```

Getting products

The object under test is the controller's scope `getAll` method. Here are the steps to call the method for a successful HTTP response:

1. For a successful HTTP response, use the builder to build a test product:

```
it('',function(){
  var testProduct = productDataBuilder().build();
});
```

2. Mock the HTTP request response to return `testProduct`:

```
$httpBackend.when('GET','/products').respond(200,
[testProduct]);
```

3. Call the object under test:

```
scope.getAll()
```

Now, the unsuccessful HTTP response requires an error response. Here are the steps for the unsuccessful HTTP request:

1. Mock the HTTP request response to return `testProduct`:

```
it('',function(){
  $httpBackend.when('GET','/products').respond(200,
  [testProduct]);
});
```

2. Call the object under test:

```
scope.getAll()
```

The HTTP response has been covered, and the next step will assert the expectation.

Asserting product data results

An assertion can be used to require that an HTTP request receives a response. The mocked `$httpBackend` property can call the `flush()` method to execute the HTTP response synchronously, so you don't have to worry about asynchronous issues. Here are the steps for the successful HTTP response expectation:

1. Flush the request:

```
$httpBackend.flush();
```

2. Expect the result variable on the `scope` object to have `testProductData`:

```
expect(scope.results[0]).toEqual(testProductData);
```

Here are the assert steps for the unsuccessful HTTP response expectation:

1. Flush the HTTP request using the following code:

   ```
   $httpBackend.flush()
   ```

2. Confirm that the scopes' error value has been set:

   ```
   expect(scope.error).toEqual('error');
   ```

Now that the tests have been assembled, the next step is to make them run.

Making the product data tests run

Here are the steps to get the controller test running:

1. Run Karma:

   ```
   $ karma start
   ```

2. The first error is `Error: [ng:areq] Argument 'ProductController' is not a function, got undefined`. To rectify this, perform the following steps:

   1. This error means that `ProductController` doesn't exist. Create a controller stub in `app/productController.js`:

      ```
      angular.module('product')
      .controller('ProductController',['$scope',function($scope){
      }]);
      ```

   2. Rerun the test.

3. This next error is `TypeError: 'undefined' is not a function (evaluating 'scope.getAll()')`. To rectify this, perform the following steps:

   1. This error means that there is no function called `getAll` in the controller. Add the function now:

      ```
      .controller('ProductController',['$scope',function($scope){
      $scope.getAll() = function(){
      };
      }]);
      ```

   2. Rerun the test.

4. The next error is `Error: No pending request to flush!`. To rectify this error, perform the following steps:

    1. This error occurs because the test is expecting an HTTP request to be flushed but there is no request. Add `productService` to `controller` so that the request will get made. Add `productService` as a dependency:

        ```
        .controller('ProductController', ['$scope','productService',
        function($scope,productService){
        ```

    2. Add `productService` to the `getAll` function:

        ```
        scope.getAll = function(){
        productService.getAll();
        };
        ```

    3. Rerun the test.

5. The next error is `Expected undefined to equal { id : 1, name : 'productName' }`. To rectify this error, perform the following steps:

    1. This error occurs because `scope.results` has not been set when the product service was successful. Add a successful callback to `productService` and set the scope's results variable:

        ```
        productService.getAll()
        .success(function(data){
        $scope.results = data;
        });
        ```

6. Now we're down to one failure, which is `Expected undefined to equal`. To rectify this, perform the following step:

    1. This error occurs because we haven't handled the error condition of the HTTP request. Add the error condition of `productService` so that it sets the scope's error:

        ```
        productService.getAll()
            .success(function(data){
              $scope.results = data;
        })
            .error(function(error){
              $scope.error = error;
        })
        ```

7. Confirm that all the tests pass now.

The unit tests for the product controller have been completed using a mocked backend to test both positive and negative scenarios. The next step can be skipped, as there were no callouts during development.

The next section will look at how to test from an end-to-end perspective.

Testing middle-to-end

Now that the unit level testing of the application is complete, the user facing tests can be worked on. One of the benefits of Angular mocks is that it provides $httpBackend, which can be used to mock data for end-to-end tests. As data is being mocked, it is really a middle-to-end test. This is because only the UI interactions are being tested, as the rest of the behavior has been mocked. This will allow us to create scaffolding for the UI layer. Once the development is complete, the scaffolding can be removed and a full end-to-end test can be put in place.

Here are the initial setup steps to create the application UI using a mocked backend with Protractor:

1. Install Protractor:

   ```
   $ npm install protractor
   ```

2. Update WebDriver:

   ```
   $ ./node_modules/protractor/bin/webdriver-manager update
   ```

3. Copy the example's Chrome-only configuration:

   ```
   $ cp ./node_modules/protractor/example/chromeOnlyConf.js .
   ```

4. Open up the chromOnlyConf.js and update the driver to point to the node_modules directory:

   ```
   chromeDriver:
   './node_modules/protractor/selenium/chromedriver',
   ```

5. Update the base URL variable:

   ```
   baseUrl: 'http://localhost:8080/',
   ```

6. Update the test directory:

   ```
   specs: ['spec/e2e/**/*.js'],
   ```

7. Add `ngMockE2e` as a dependency to the product module in the app or `product.js` file:

```
angular.module('product',['ngMockE2e'])
```

8. Set up the mock request:

```
.run(['$httpBackend',function($httpBackend) {
        var testProduct = productDataBuilder().build();
var products = [testProduct];
        $httpBackend.whenGET('/products').respond(products);
}]);
```

9. Create the `index.html` page using an HTML stub:

```
<!DOCTYPE html>
<html>
<head>
        <title></title>
</head>
<body>
</body>
</html>
```

10. Add the AngularJS references:

```
<script src="bower_components/angular/angular.js"></script>
</body>
```

11. Add the product module, controller, and service:

```
<script src="app/product.js"></script>
<script src="app/productService.js"></script>
<script src="app/productController.js"></script>
```

12. For mocking purposes, add Angular mocks and the product data builder:

```
<script src="bower_components/angular-mocks/angular-mocks.js"></script>
<script src="spec/productDataBuilder.js"></script>
```

The initial's index page and mock has been set up. The next step will walk through the TDD life cycle and get the application rocking.

Test first

The first step in the life cycle is to create the tests using the 3 A's. The test confirms that the product data will be visible on the page once a user pushes a button to get the product data.

Assembling the product test

Here are the steps to assemble the Protractor test:

1. Create a new file for the test called `spec/e2e/productScenario.js`:

    ```
    $ touch productScenario.js
    ```

2. Create the test stub:

    ```
    describe('',function(){
      beforeEach(function(){
      });
      it('',function(){
      });
    });
    ```

3. Browse the application:

    ```
    beforeEach(function(){
      browser.get('/index.html');
    });
    ```

4. Find the button that we will be selecting:

    ```
    beforeEach(function(){
      var productButton = element(by.buttonText
    ('Get Products'));
    });
    ```

Now that the test has been assembled, we can hit the object under test.

Getting products

The action of this test is to select the product button. As we have already retrieved the button in the Assemble section, we can now click on it:

```
beforeEach(function(){
var productButton = element(by.buttonText('Get Products'));
productButton.click();
});
```

Finally, it is time to create the assertions and expectations.

Expecting product data results

The assertion for this test is to ensure that the product data is now displayed. Here are the steps:

1. Find the results:

   ```
   var results = element.all(by.repeater
   ('result in results'));
   ```

2. Assert that the count is greater than 0:

   ```
   expect(results.count()).toBeGreaterThan(0);
   ```

The test setup is complete. The next step is to make it run.

Making the product data run

As has been done with the other Protractor tests, one process will be running the HTTP page and the other will be running the protractor test:

1. Install `http-server` so that we can run the website:

   ```
   $ npm install http-server
   ```

2. Start the website:

   ```
   $ ./node_modules/http-server/bin/http-server .
   ```

3. In another command window, run the protractor tests:

   ```
   $ ./node_modules/protractor/bin/protractor chromeOnlyConf.js
   ```

4. The first error is `Error: Angular could not be found on the page http://localhost:8080/index.html : angular never provided resumeBootstrap`. To rectify this, perform the following steps:

   1. The preceding error is due to the fact that we haven't referenced the application module in the web page. Add the product module to the body of the application:

      ```
      <body ng-app='product'>
      ```

   2. Rerun the tests.

5. The next error is `NoSuchElementError: No element found using locator: by.buttonText("Get Products")`. To rectify this, perform the following step:

   1. Add the button:

      ```
      <button>Get Products</button>
      ```

6. The next error has hit the expectation and states `Expected 0 to be greater than 0`. To fix this, we need to first add `productController` to the page:

```
<div ng-controller='ProductController'>
  <button>Get Products</button>
</div>
```

7. The next step is to associate the button-click with the `ProductController` classes scope to get all products:

```
<button ng-click='getAll()'>Get Products</button>
```

8. The final step is to display all results:

```
<div ng-repeat="result in results">
  {{result}}
</div>
```

The test now shows a successful result.

The *make it better* step will be skipped as there is nothing immediate that needs to be refactored. At this point, the application is tested and operated using the mocked data. You should be able to see how powerful this technique can be as you're building up an application. The next section will look at removing the scaffolding and using an actual backend.

Testing end-to-end

Remove the Angular mocks scaffolding and set up the test to actually connect to the real server and setup.

The backend of Angular mocks allowed us to create the application without the need to actually return data. Now that the application has been set up, we can remove the scaffolding and create a real HTTP request for the data. Here are the steps:

1. Remove `ngMockE2e` and the mock response from the products module in `app/product.js`:

```
angular.module('product',[]);
Remove Angular mocks and productDataBuilder from the
index.html page
```

2. Rerun the Protractor test.

3. The error states the failed expectation.

Now that the mock HTTP response has been removed, we need to add an actual request. Luckily for us, we don't have to use any other tool or framework and can use the `http-server` module that we have been using the whole time. In a real-world example, the product route would live in a separate service, but this example will use a simpler approach for brevity.

Getting the product data

The `http-server` module, which is used to serve static content, can be extended to serve static content as well. This allows us to set up a static file that mirrors a request route. In this case, a single JSON file of products will be used. The products file will have an array of product data. Here are the steps:

1. Create a new file named `products` in the root of the project:

   ```
   $ touch products
   ```

2. Open the file and add the following content:

   ```
   [{
     "id": 1,
     "name": "productName"
   }]
   ```

Now, the `/products` route is available and will return an array of products. Rerun the Protractor test, and confirm that it is passing. With these simple tests, we have tested the application end-to-end and successfully removed the mock scaffolding.

This concludes the walk-through of using TDD to create an AngularJS REST layer.

Self-test questions

Q1. A callback function refers to a function that is called after an asynchronous function completes.

1. True
2. False

Q2. An `XMLHttpRequest` cannot send or receive JSON.

1. True
2. False

Q3. REST stands for:

1. Representational State Transfer
2. Nothing
3. Repeatable Endpoint State Transfer

Q4. Asynchronous functions always complete in the order in which they were called.

1. True
2. False

Q5. There are two different implementations of `$httpBackend`: one for unit and one for end-to-end testing.

1. True
2. False

Summary

This chapter explained the details behind REST requests, asynchronous testing, and the mocking of Angular HTTP requests in Karma and Protractor. It has brought together many of the techniques and tools used throughout the book. Specifically, it has showed us how to apply the TDD life cycle (test first, make it run, and make it better) to incrementally build your applications to a specification and how to use the 3A's (Assemble, Act, and Assert) to construct a test.

As you complete this book and go about applying the techniques in the real world, remember that knowing what to test is just as important as knowing how to test. This book has shown you how; it is up to you to practice and continue to improve your development skills through TDD.

A
Integrating Selenium Server with Protractor

Throughout this book, we used Selenium ChromeDriver to test with Protractor. What this meant was that in order to run a Protractor test, we simply had to have the website running and then kick off Protractor. In *Chapter 3, End-to-end Testing with Protractor*, ChromeDriver was installed and used to run the tests. From the perspective of the book and TDD, this was acceptable. Our tests were small and contained and did not have a lot of moving parts.

The problem with only using ChromeDriver is that we can't test on other browsers. As your application grows and you want to support more browsers, you need to think about running a standalone Selenium Server. This section of the book provides a walk-through of how to get a standalone Selenium Server running and integrated with Protractor.

Installation

The good thing about installation is that we have already done it before. Every time we installed ChromeDriver, the first thing we did was install Selenium. Here are the standard steps:

1. Install the Protractor npm module:

    ```
    $ npm install protractor
    ```

2. Install Selenium WebDriver:

    ```
    $ ./node_modules/protractor/bin/webdriver-manager update
    ```

That's it. Selenium is now installed and is ready to be used. In the next section, we will see how to update the Protractor configuration to use the Selenium standalone server.

Protractor configuration

Luckily for us, we don't have to remember all the basic configurations for Protractor. Within `npm_modules`, there are examples that we can use. Here are the steps to copy the Selenium standalone configuration:

1. Open up the example Protractor configuration file that is located in the following directory:

    `./node_modules/protractor/example/conf.js`

2. Copy the file to your local test folder:

    `$ cp ./node_modules/protractor/example/conf.js`

The configuration should look very similar to the `chromeOnly` configuration. Here is a snippet of the important configuration items:

```
exports.config = {
  seleniumAddress: 'http://localhost:4444/wd/hub',

  capabilities: {
    'browserName': 'chrome'
  },
  ...
};
```

The first important item is the `seleniumAddress` object. The address is the hostname, port, and location where the Selenium Server is running. The next important item is the `capabilities` object. Browser-specific capabilities give you the ability to define which browsers will be tested against. As we are not using the `ChromeOnly` configuration, you can now choose **Internet Explorer (IE)**, Firefox, and so on. For more information on multiple browser support and capabilities, refer to the Protractor documentation at `https://github.com/angular/protractor/blob/master/docs/browser-setup.md`

In the next section, we will look at how to run Selenium.

> The `seleniumAddress` object is meant to be configurable so that you can have a separate instance in a completely different location than your development machine. Visit the Selenium site for more information at `http://www.seleniumhq.org/`.

Running Selenium

Selenium is quite straightforward to start. Once run, it can just sit in the background while the tests are running:

1. Start the Selenium standalone service:

    ```
    $ ./node_modules/protractor/bin/webdriver-manager start
    ```

2. The console window will display several information messages. Ensure the following messages are displayed:

    ```
    $ ./node_modules/protractor/bin/webdriver-manager start
    seleniumProcess.pid: 13820
    13:39:59.882 INFO - Launching a standalone server

    13:40:00.250 INFO - Java: Oracle Corporation 24.45-b08
    13:40:00.250 INFO - OS: Windows 7 6.1 amd64
    13:40:00.267 INFO - v2.43.1, with Core v2.43.1. Built from revision 5163bce
    13:40:00.401 INFO - RemoteWebDriver instances should connect to: http://127.0.0.1:4444/wd/hub
    13:40:00.403 INFO - Version Jetty/5.1.x
    13:40:00.404 INFO - Started HttpContext[/selenium-server/driver,/selenium-server/driver]
    13:40:00.407 INFO - Started HttpContext[/selenium-server,/selenium-server]
    13:40:00.408 INFO - Started HttpContext[/,/]
    13:40:00.476 INFO - Started org.openqa.jetty.jetty.servlet.ServletHandler@2f375701
    13:40:00.476 INFO - Started HttpContext[/wd,/wd]
    13:40:00.487 INFO - Started SocketListener on 0.0.0.0:4444
    13:40:00.488 INFO - Started org.openqa.jetty.jetty.Server@1728cbe6
    ```

3. You should ensure that the default port used, as can be seen in the `RemoteWebDriver` message in the preceding messages, is the same as the one that is configured in the Protractor configuration:

    ```
    seleniumAddress: 'http://localhost:4444/wd/hub',
    ...
    ```

Let it run

Selenium is now running on the `4444` localhost port. In order to ensure that Protractor can communicate with Selenium, let's run a simple test to ensure everything is working. As we have done throughout the book, we will follow the TDD steps even though this will be an extremely short and simple test. As Protractor is installed, the only other prerequisite is to install an HTTP server. Install `http-server` using the following command:

```
$ npm install http-server
```

Once it is installed, start the server:

```
$ ./node_modules/http-server/bin/http-server
```

Test first

The test will check whether the title of the page is equal to `seleniumTestTitle`. Create a new Protractor test file named `scenario.js`.

Assemble

To set up the test, we need to navigate the browser to the root of the web application:

```
beforeEach(function(){
  browser.get("/");
});
```

There is no Act section as we will simply be checking that the loaded index page has the title we need.

Assert

The assert needs get the title and compare it with the expected value:

```
it('',function(){
  expect(browser.getTitle()).toBe('seleniumTestTitle');
});
```

Make it run

Now that the test is prepared, we can start running the Protractor test through the standalone Selenium Server. Here are the steps to run the Protractor test:

1. Add the test file to the Protractor configuration:

    ```
    specs: ['scenario.js'],
    ```

2. Create an empty HTML page that will be used to make the test run:

```
<!DOCTYPE html>
<html>
<head>
  <title></title>
</head>
<body>

</body>
</html>
```

3. Add the index page to the Protractor configuration:

```
specs: ['scenario.js','index.html'],
```

4. Run the test:

```
$ ./node-modules/protractor/bin/protractor conf.js
```

5. The first error is **Angular could not be found on the page http://localhost:8080/index.html : retries looking for angular exceeded**. To rectify this, perform the following steps:

   1. AngularJS has not been added to the page. Install `angular` through `bower`:

      ```
      $ bower install angular
      ```

   2. Add the AngularJS reference to the `index.html` page:

      ```
      <script type="text/javascript"
        src="bower_components/angular/angular.js"></script>
      ```

   3. Rerun the test.

6. The next error is **Angular could not be found on the page http://localhost:8080/index.html : angular never provided resumeBootstrap**. This error means that AngularJS couldn't load the main module of your application. To rectify this, perform the following steps:

   1. Add a simple module into the `body` tag:

      ```
      <body ng-app='test'>
      ```

   2. Initialize the module in the last tag:

      ```
      <script type="text/javascript"
      src="bower_components/angular/angular.js"></script>
      <script type="text/javascript">
        angular.module('test',[]);
      </script>
      ```

   3. Rerun the test.

7. The next error has hit the expectation: **Expected 'http://localhost:8080/index. html' to be 'seleniumTestTitle'**. Here are the steps to rectify this error:

    1. Set the title of the web page to the expectation:

        ```
        <title>seleniumTestTitle</title>
        ```

    2. Rerun the test.

8. The Protractor output now reports **1 test, 1 assertion, 0 failures**. With the success of the test, we have now successfully shown you how to use the Selenium standalone server.

Summary

This appendix has shown you how to set up and use the Selenium standalone server. There are many options and advantages of using the standalone server. The advantages are geared more for advanced testing when you want to use a dedicated Selenium Server or a PaaS (Platform as a Service) or if you want to test a functionality on different browsers and as the volume of your Protractor tests grow. For more information, visit the Selenium home page at `http://www.seleniumhq.org/`.

B
Automating Karma Unit Testing on Commit

Running tests locally is one thing, but how do you know whether they will work on someone else's computer. Setting up continuous testing and integration should be part of every application you write. One of the best things is that the tools to set up are free, easy to use, and best of all, they get to showcase your tests! The following section will explore how to set up continuous integration using GitHub for source control and Travis for continuous integration.

GitHub

GitHub is a source control, collaboration, and all-around awesome tool. For open source projects, it is free. Once you sign up, you can get started and create a new repository for your project. GitHub provides a Git URL for every project; the URL can then be set up to push changes like any other Git repository. One of the benefits of using GitHub is that it automatically provides hooks into other applications and services. When setting up continuous integration and testing through Travis CI, you will leverage the Travis CI GitHub hook.

Test setup

In order to run Karma properly, we will need to add the following development dependencies:

- `karma`: The base Karma installation
- `karma-jasmine`: The test runner
- `karma-phantomjs-launcher`: The PhantomJS headless browser plugin we discussed and set up in *Chapter 5*, *Flip Flop*

Install the following Karma dev dependencies:

```
$ npm install karma --save-dev
$ npm install karma-jasmine --save-dev
$ npm install karma-phantomjs-launcher --save-dev
```

Test scripts

When using Travis CI, a script to run the tests needs to be defined. The best place to define a script is in the `package.json` file. The `package.json` file is used in several ways by `node.js`. Here are the steps to run the test:

1. The test script can then be run when you type the following command in the command prompt:

   ```
   $ npm test
   ```

2. Update the `package.json` scripts section as shown in the following code snippet:

   ```
   "scripts": {
       "start": "node app.js",
       "test" : "karma start --single-run --browsers PhantomJS"
   }
   ```

3. Confirm that the test script works:

   ```
   $ npm test
   ```

PhantomJS allows tests to run on the Travis CI servers without the need for a UI. The following is a sample output:

The application setup is now configured to run unit tests via the `npm test` command. This will be used by Travis CI to run the tests.

Setting the hook

GitHub provides several hooks into other applications. A hook allows you to chain actions when a commit occurs. A hook is an extremely useful feature from a continuous integration standpoint because we can set up the code to be tested on every commit. Travis CI has a GitHub hook that can be easily set up on any GitHub repository. The following is a walk-through on how to create a Travis CI hook on your open source repository.

Creating the hook

Here are the steps to create the hook:

1. Create a Travis CI account by going to the Travis CI page at `https://travis-ci.org` and click on **Sign in with GitHub**. Confirm the questions it asks and continue.

2. Activate a GitHub Webhook to Travis CI. You can set up the Webhook in Travis CI through your profile URL at `https://travis-ci.org/profile`

3. Turn the switch on. In the profile, you should see your repository.

   ° Here is a before view of Webhook (Switch off):

   tjchaplin/the-mean-way   OFF

   ° Here is a view of the Webhook after it is enabled(Switch on):

```
$ npm test


> karma start --single-run --browsers PhantomJS

INFO [karma]: Karma v0.12.16 server started at http://localhost:9876/
INFO [launcher]: Starting browser PhantomJS
INFO [PhantomJS 1.9.7 (Windows 7)]: Connected on socket aCuNNhmOONiqwytBkmzx wit
h id 72833197
PhantomJS 1.9.7 (Windows 7): Executed 3 of 3 SUCCESS (0.013 secs / 0.014 secs)
```

Adding a Travis configuration file

Travis requires a configuration file to be at the root of your repository named `.travis.yml`. The configuration file contains the source code language, language versioning, metadata, and other information. The template configuration will look as follows:

```
language: node_js
node_js:
  - "0.10"
```

Besides the basic configuration in the preceding code, additional setup is needed to run Karma tests. The `before_script` configuration will be used to install Karma and Bower prior to running any tests. Here is what the configuration needs to look like in order to install Karma and Bower before any tests run:

```
language: node_js
node_js:
  - "0.10"
```

```
before_script:
  - npm install -g karma-cli
  - npm install -g bower
  - bower install
```

Now the tests are ready to be run. Add the preceding contents to a new file named `travis.yml`. By default, the `Node.js` project will execute the `npm test` command in Travis. This is why you don't need to specify the actual command to test your application.

> Please note that Travis CI is case sensitive.

The following screenshot is an example of what the preceding code looks like:

If you have any issues, go to the Travis CI **Getting started** guide at `http://docs.travis-ci.com/user/getting-started/`.

References

The following are some references that may help you with the concepts:

- This form of user specification is written using the Gerkin syntax. The Gerkin syntax allows you to write the specifications in a well-formatted manner. See the following link for more details: `http://en.wikipedia.org/wiki/Behavior-driven_development`.

- The JavaScript Jabber homepage can be found at `http://javascriptjabber.com/106-jsj-protractor-with-julie-ralph/`

- The GitHub page for `http-server` can be found at `https://github.com/nodeapps/http-server`

C
Answers

Chapter 1, Introduction to Test-driven Development

Q1	2
Q2	1
Q3	1
Q4	1
Q5	2

Chapter 2, The Karma Way

Q1	2
Q2	2
Q3	2
Q4	2

Chapter 3, End-to-end Testing with Protractor

Q1	1
Q2	1
Q3	1

Chapter 4, The First Step

Q1	1
Q2	2
Q3	1

Chapter 5, Flip Flop

Q1	3
Q2	3
Q3	1

Chapter 6, Telling the World

Q1	2
Q2	1
Q3	1

Chapter 7, Give Me Some Data

Q1	1
Q2	2
Q3	1
Q4	2
Q5	1

Index

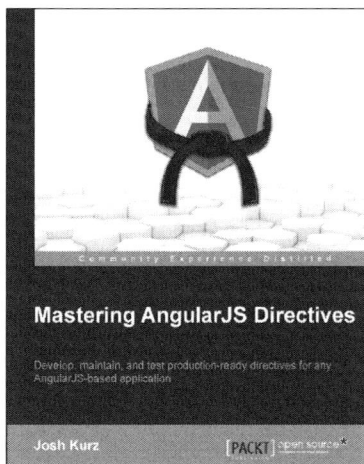

Mastering AngularJS Directives

ISBN: 978-1-78398-158-8   Paperback: 210 pages

Develop, maintain, and test production-ready directives for any AngularJS-based application

1. Explore the options available for creating directives, by reviewing detailed explanations and real-world examples.

2. Dissect the life cycle of a directive and understand why they are the base of the AngularJS framework.

3. Discover how to create structured, maintainable, and testable directives through a step-by-step, hands-on approach to AngularJS.

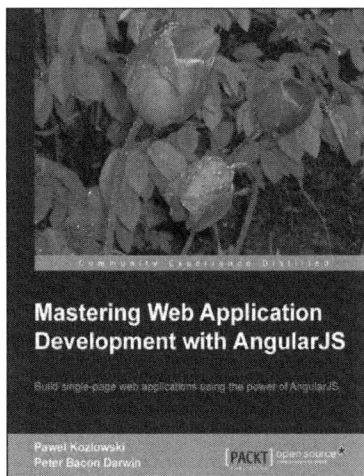

Mastering Web Application Development with AngularJS

ISBN: 978-1-78216-182-0   Paperback: 372 pages

Build single-page web applications using the power of AngularJS

1. Make the most out of AngularJS by understanding the AngularJS philosophy and applying it to real-life development tasks.

2. Effectively structure, write, test, and finally deploy your application.

3. Add security and optimization features to your AngularJS applications.

Please check **www.PacktPub.com** for information on our titles

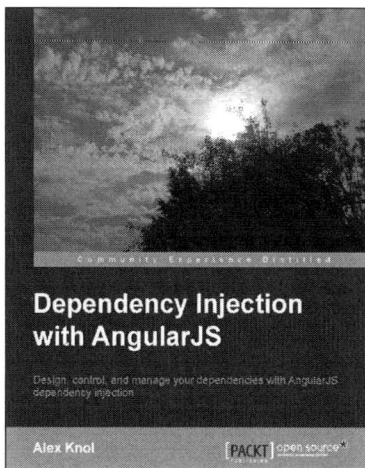

Dependency Injection with AngularJS

ISBN: 978-1-78216-656-6   Paperback: 78 pages

Design, control, and manage your dependencies with AngularJS dependency injection

1. Understand the concept of dependency injection.

2. Isolate units of code during testing JavaScript using Jasmine.

3. Create reusable components in AngularJS.

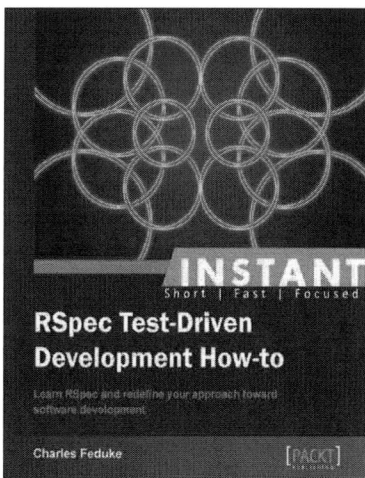

Instant RSpec Test-Driven Development How-to

ISBN: 978-1-78216-522-4   Paperback: 68 pages

Learn RSpec and redefine your approach towards software development

1. Learn something new in an Instant! A short, fast, focused guide delivering immediate results.

2. Learn how to use RSpec with Rails.

3. Easy to read and grok examples.

4. Write idiomatic specifications.

Please check **www.PacktPub.com** for information on our titles

13562806R00115

Printed in Great Britain
by Amazon.co.uk, Ltd.,
Marston Gate.